Autistic children

Original Titles:

Order and Obey (1933)

....

Language and Emotional Connection (1943)

....

Autism in Childhood: An Attempt of an Analysis (1957)

by Dr. George Frankl

Edition, Translation and Comments:

Dr. Kevin Rebecchi, PhD

TABLE OF CONTENTS

FOREWORD

The edition and translations of the four articles (1934a, 1934b, 1943, 1957), "Order and Obey: a pedagogical study; Part I," "Order and Obey: a pedagogical study; Part II," "Language and affective contact," and "Autism in Childhood: An Attempt of an Analysis" by George Frankl have never been published as a book - unless I am mistaken. Just like the texts of Hans Asperger (Rebecchi, 2023a), Grounia Iefimovna Sukhareva (Rebecchi, 2022), Leo Kanner (Rebecchi, 2023b), and Lorna Wing (Rebecchi, 2023c) it seemed essential to circulate these essential and foundational texts in the contemporary conception of autism.

This translation and edition will allow people to form their own opinion on George Frankl's statements and help those already sensitized to the subject to better understand the concept of neurodiversity (understood as the neurobiological and psychological variation of the human species, similar to variations in skin color, height, or intelligence). It will also provide a better grasp of the historical background of contemporary autism conception. This edition and translation can shed light on the fact that language peculiarities in autism (which Frankl refers to as a disorder of affective language) are not as clear-cut and caricatural as some assert, and their characterization (especially through the notions of deficit and disorder) is never devoid of a socio-cultural context and environment. We have long witnessed a phenomenon of pathologizing difference, which is why it appears necessary and imperative to study the past.

Although George Frankl did not formally and explicitly discuss autism before his 1957 text, readers will have the opportunity to find numerous parallels and similarities with the texts of Asperger and Kanner concerning psychology, manifestations, cognitive abilities, and communication of individuals with autism. Furthermore, the presence of these various texts allows for a better understanding of his intellectual journey. Robison (2017) from William & Mary University in Maryland, USA, and Muratori and colleagues from the University of Pisa in Italy (2019, 2021) notably highlight the strong influence he had on them. Hence, his work adds significant value to the debate, particularly as he was one of the first to speak of a continuum (or spectrum) and autistic conditions.

In contrast to Hans Asperger, Grunya Efimovna Sukhareva, and Leo Kanner, George Frankl does not describe singular "behaviors," but rather, he describes a unique language system specific to autism. Understanding and studying this language system are crucial for better comprehension of individuals with autism, effective communication with them, and dispelling certain preconceptions on the subject.

As I mentioned in the prefaces of the editions and translations of Leo Kanner, Hans Asperger, Lorna Wing, and Grounia Iefimovna Sukhareva, providing a simple definition of autism is not easy. In a broad sense, it refers to a different relationship with the world and others, leading to perceiving and experiencing differently, thinking and analyzing differently, and ultimately acting and behaving (and hence communicating) differently from the majority and established norms. As a result, individuals with autism are often labeled as strange, peculiar, unique, not enough, or even too much.

Therefore, it was important for me to make these texts accessible to the general public, and I will further develop some of Frankl's descriptions and ideas in the afterword.

References

Frankl, G. (1934a). Befehlen und Gehorchen : eine heilpädagogische Studie. Teil I. Zeitschrift für Kinderforschung, 42(3), 463-479.

Frankl, G. (1934b). Befehlen und Gehorchen : eine heilpädagogische Studie; Teil II. Zeitschrift für Kinderforschung 43(1), 1-21.

Frankl, G. (1943). Language and affective contact. Nervous Child 2(3), 251–262.

Frankl, G. (1957). Autism in Childhood: An Attempt of an Analysis (unpublished manuscript). Lawrence, KS: Kenneth Spencer Research Library, The University of Kansas.

Muratori, F., & Bizzari, V. (2019). Autism as a Disruption of Affective Contact: The Forgotten Role of George Frankl. Clinical neuropsychiatry, 16(4), 159–164.

Muratori, F., Calderoni, S., & Bizzari, V. (2021). George Frankl: an undervalued voice in the history of autism. European child &

adolescent psychiatry, 30(8), 1273–1280. https://doi.org/10.1007/s00787-020-01622-4

Rebecchi, K. (2022). Autistic children: Grunya Sukhareva. Kindle Direct Publishing.

Rebecchi, K. (2023a). Autistic children: Hans Asperger. Kindle Direct Publishing.

Rebecchi, K. (2023b). Autistic children: Leo Kanner. Kindle Direct Publishing.

Rebecchi, K. (2023c). Autistic children: Lorna Wing. Kindle Direct Publishing.

Robison J. E. (2017). Kanner, Asperger, and Frankl: A third man at the genesis of the autism diagnosis. Autism: the international journal of research and practice, 21(7), 862–871. https://doi.org/10.1177/1362361316654283

ORDER AND OBEY: A STUDY OF CURATIVE PEDAGOGY (1933)

PART I

During a lunch at an inn, I had the opportunity to witness two dogs demonstrating very clearly how an order can be given correctly and how it can be given incorrectly. Both dogs were supposed to keep their master company during the meal. One of them, a lively and nervous Fox, constantly begged its mistress by whimpering and howling. However, she gently and lovingly persuaded him to rest and lie down. She assured him that he would have his meal later and asked him to behave as a good dog should. But she spoke in such a calm, amiable, and unimposing voice that it had no effect on him. After all, a dog can only imperfectly understand such a monotonous speech. Therefore, she had to throw him a piece of food from time to time, which encouraged him to beg even more.

The other dog, a considerably large German Boxer, was also well-loved and well-treated by its owner. But a simple "Lie down!" was enough to make him rest in a corner throughout the meal. This command had the necessary suggestive power; it was delivered in the right tone, energetic and authoritative - not unfriendly - and accompanied by the corresponding gesture. The will and strength to enforce the order must undoubtedly have been perceived by the dog. Certainly, good training was a prerequisite for his obedience, but he would certainly not have followed if the lady had spoken to him in her kind yet expressionless manner.

This scene stayed vividly in my memory because shortly after, I observed a similar one between a young child and his mother.

The boy was five years old, particularly restless, noisy, and had difficulty concentrating. As later confirmed at the clinic, he was particularly responsive to the suggestive power of penetrating language. It was with this child that his mother, an elderly and very abnormal woman, came to our outpatient service. The boy behaved very badly, being everywhere he shouldn't and misbehaving in various ways. But the mother, slow and irritated, crept behind him and spoke in a monotonous voice with an expressionless face, saying, "My dear, you really have to stop this, or I'll get angry, sit down now. Look at how well-behaved the other children are." And so on, in a moralizing tone. In principle, it was the same as in the scene between the lady and her Fox. The boy hardly perceived these feeble words, and even if he did, he was not compelled to do what was asked of him.

The scenes I have just described are glaring examples of inappropriate and, therefore, erroneous orders. No one should conclude from this that it is wrong and inappropriate to give affectionate advice in all circumstances and to any child, nor is it always necessary to choose the form of a brief and energetic command when trying to get something from a child. Both forms can be considered right or wrong. It is now necessary to examine the conditions upon which the correct use of one or the other form depends.

One thing becomes immediately evident: there are not just two opposing ways of giving orders, namely the choice between energy and gentleness, but also an infinite number of variations and nuances. To be convinced of this, one only needs to imagine the same order in its various possible forms. Let's take the example of the series of orders derived from the indifferent imperative form "Come here." There are the energetic expressions "Will you please come here?" and "You are going to come here soon!", the objective command "Come here!", the urgent and repetitive command "Come now," the conciliatory request "Would you be kind enough to come here?", and the "Come here, so that..." justifying the necessity! The series could go on infinitely. Different dialects are particularly rich in modifications of this type, often very drastic and expressive.

Despite their identical factual content, all these expressions seem very different from one another. By changing the order of the sentence, modifying the verb tense, or adding various adverbs or affective expressions, they acquire very different shades, all with the same purpose. These are the countless feelings, emotions, dispositions, expectations, and desires that accompany the expression and are generally expressed only in this way and not in words: kindness, love, compliance, good will, anger, indifference, threat, request, supplication, urgency, excitement, and so on.

However, even the differentiated forms of orders are not yet clearly defined by their grammatical structure alone as presented in writing. It is only by imagining the intonation, gestures, and expressions that accompany the order that it becomes clear to the viewer or recipient. For example, the expression "Are you finally going to come here?" could mean at times a final warning before punishment, at other times an indignant exclamation or a resigned sigh of despair, sometimes a repetition of previous orders, and yet sometimes a playful exclamation from an adult interacting with a young child. Even the undifferentiated expression "Come here!" is itself considered completely indeterminate in its emotional content and can mean an infinite number of things. However, as soon as it is accompanied by a certain form of expression, a specific intonation, and a certain interplay of expressions and gestures, it becomes clearly determined in its emotional content. This applies not only to orders but everywhere in human relationships where objective communication is used to express various emotional moments.

It might momentarily seem that it is up to the educator's discretion to choose, from this vast arsenal of countless variations available for each order by modifying its emotional content, the one that best aligns with their pedagogical principles. One may decide to always speak to their students with love, another to explain everything they must do in a cold and rational manner as necessary, while a third might prefer to consistently use a concise commanding tone.

It is evident that this is impossible. The most significant obstacle lies, however, in the educator themselves, who, in a life situation, cannot behave towards the child according to their own free appreciation, as dictated by their reason or preconceived opinion. Instead, they depend on their own personality, experience, and feelings. What they express through their expressions, gestures, and word emphasis can only be their own feelings, what they truly and directly experience in the moment. The child should not see gestures of kindness or anger, but rather the person who is genuinely angry or kind, evoking genuine fear or affection. It is not possible, or at least not correct, to display any feelings foreign to one's own personality that have never been felt as a natural and naive human being. Such foreign, imitated, or adopted behaviors appear false, affected, or ridiculous. The child's instinct rightly draws conclusions from this: they do not fear a threat they recognize as feigned and do not respond at all to simulated kindness, or they respond with rejection.

The countless possibilities for variation in the form of orders are limited by the character of the child to whom the order is given. Let's imagine an educator in contact with children of different characters, giving each of them an order with the same material content. The educator has a certain perception of each child: for example, they see a sensitive and timid girl, then a robust and lively boy, a spirited child, and another who is rather calm and passive, a child who believes in authority, and another who is assertive. Depending on their age, gender, different personality traits, experiences, and encounters they had with them and similar children, they possess an extremely complex idea of each child's personality and psychic life. When giving an order, they can't express just any feelings from their emotional repertoire, but only those they specifically feel towards that particular child. This is an extraordinarily fine adaptation, partly governed by instinct and partly by reason. It would be impossible to address a cheerful child in the same way as a sad child, a fearful child in the same way as a bold child, and so on. If one were to address a three-year-old child in the same way as an adult or even an older child, it would seem very awkward or ridiculous.

It seems important to discuss the following points: When

giving orders and generally interacting with a child, one does not adapt to the child's real and effective character but only to the one perceived by the educator themselves. If, in the educator's eyes, a child is endowed with qualities they do not actually possess, or if one of their reactions is misunderstood, it automatically results in an erroneous emotional attitude towards the child, which is expressed in educational measures and, above all, in their emotional content. Therefore, any change in the educator's opinion of the child leads to a change or a new nuance in their behavior towards the child. Each new diagnostic progress, each recognition of a new characteristic of the being, each correction of an error about it modifies the child in their eyes in one direction or another and thus also the feelings they have for the child. In certain circumstances, they see the child differently from how they previously saw them and are compelled to approach the child differently at that moment.

This plays an important role in questions of educational advice. When providing educational advice to parents or educators concerning certain children, one is generally ready to instruct them on how to do things differently than before or how they should behave with the child in particular circumstances. Any slightly experienced and critical education advisor knows how rarely such advice finds a receptive ear. Parents always see specific characteristics, good or bad, behind the child's reactions, which automatically leads to a certain emotional attitude. Therefore, as long as the child's reactions are misunderstood, educational measures will also be erroneous, at least in terms of their emotional content. Even the best advice will not change this unless the advisor chooses the most practical path and uses their diagnostic knowledge to help parents understand the nature of their child, especially in their difficulties. When a striking or unpleasant reaction from a child is understood in its mechanism, the educator's natural instinct generally has no difficulty in finding the right therapeutic response. Many examples of this are provided in this book.

If we assume, in accordance with the two restrictions established so far, a well-defined and well-known educator's personality, and a similarly well-known child in their essence, and now we must imagine how this educator says "Come here" to this child, we are still in a quandary. One could imagine a whole series of possible nuances in the tone of communication, all of which could be adapted to the existing emotional relationship between the two and, under certain circumstances, be correct. It is only by imagining a very specific situation between them that we can answer this question. For example, I can imagine a child crying on their first night in the service due to homesickness and a sense of abandonment, and the educator calling them over to distract them from their pain. The form in which they do so, the way they express their compassion and understanding of the pain while quickly trying to move on to another topic, seems almost evident to me, given my knowledge of the two personalities and the presented situation.

It turns out that the freedom of the educator is not as extensive as it might have seemed at first, given the countless possibilities for variations offered by the language of emotions. These variations only represent an immense adaptability to the demands of the current situation. What should happen is certainly left largely to the educator's will, but not the form in which they aspire to it. Just imagine the same educator with the same children in the different situations that repeat regularly throughout the day. They must constantly change their behavior, tone, when waking the children up in the morning and helping them dress, when giving orders during gymnastics, adopting an impersonal and didactic tone during classes, and when participating in games and having fun with them. A constant change in behavior is necessary. Just as the child's mood constantly changes, the educator must also take an emotional stance and express this stance, either by accompanying and encouraging or by inhibiting and forbidding. Whatever they do and how they do it must organically integrate into the situation if they want the children to truly understand and recognize them.

It would be tempting to write a chapter about educators who do not master this emotional language in their educational measures and, therefore, do not find the right emotional connection with their students. The mother mentioned at the beginning is an extreme example of this. However, the discussion of bad educational attitudes falls more within the realm of general pedagogy, which deals with the general principles of correct education and the fundamental shortcomings of these principles, rather than therapeutic pedagogy. Regardless of the endogenous or exogenous causes of such pedagogical errors, whether it be a primary instinctual weakness, inhibition due to fear and insecurity towards the child, or inhibition due to principles leading to a petrified and unnatural attitude towards children, the effects are always similar. Educational measures taken by such educators have a singularly empty, unbinding, and unimpressive effect, not only on the children but also on an unrelated observer. One gets the impression that they are not adapted to the situation. They are either too loud or too silent, too severe in their commands or too tearful. Or a too violent and not entirely justified anger suddenly arises from intended indulgence, and the educator is carried away by this anger. These emotionally inaccurate orders have no positive effect on the children, and they do not feel inclined to follow them. If such an inadequate educator is relatively weak, they risk not being respected, and conflicts are constant as the children easily get angry under their direction. On the contrary, if such an inadequate educator is very strong and energetic, they cannot create a good atmosphere among the children at all because their energy, applied discordantly, creates too rigid discipline that leaves no freedom of movement for the children.

The counterpart of such a disruption of emotional contact in the order, the same disruption in the child's obedience, belongs even more to the domain of therapeutic pedagogy. An incorrect and incomprehensible reaction of a child to a correctly given educational measure should objectively manifest as an educational difficulty. This is not about consequences or lack of consequences. The educator expects more than mere obedience in response to their order; they expect a reaction that indicates a complete and sensitive understanding of the given order, not only from a material perspective but also from an emotional perspective. If a child behaves correctly in this regard, it seems so natural and evident that no one particularly takes note of this positive quality of the child. Just as education appears particularly easy and natural with a good and well-adapted educator. It is then an ordinary, harmonious, and natural relationship, in which the adult directs and sets the tone while the child is more passive and can be largely guided and stimulated. This becomes more striking when it turns out that the child understands the words but not the emotional content of an order or when the contact between the educator and the student is suddenly broken, so the child is unable to react appropriately.

This phenomenon will first be illustrated by a case and then systematically discussed in its different forms.

Case 1 : Alfred P. (excerpt from the anamnesis)

This eleven-year-old boy, a first-year high school student, was referred by his teachers to the outpatient therapeutic pedagogy service due to his disruptive behavior at school. The purpose was to evaluate his mental state and assess his suitability for schooling.

During a meeting with the school principal and several of his main teachers, it was revealed that they would all be very happy if he were removed from the class, and the only reason they hadn't requested his expulsion yet was that they considered him abnormal rather than malicious. Nonetheless, they all complained a lot about his behavior. He didn't pay attention, didn't participate in class, and consequently couldn't keep up despite his good abilities. He was particularly restless and completely unresponsive to influence. He almost never stayed still during class, behaving in a completely careless and relentless manner. He continuously spoke, shouted, and made interjections. It was impossible to maintain discipline in class in his presence. Warnings, punishments, and even friendly advice were ineffective. It was always necessary to isolate him in the principal's office to restore calm to both him and the class.

What concerned the teachers most was his anger. They all reported that he would suddenly and ruthlessly get angry for the most trivial reasons, both during recess and class time. They feared that the boy might seriously harm a classmate with some tool, such as the tip of a compass or a pocket knife, on such an occasion.

On the other hand, the teachers always emphasized that he was kind and decent and apparently had no malicious intent in his unpleasant actions.

At home, it was easier to get along with him. The parents had little to reproach themselves for. At most, they needed to repeat their wishes several times. However, the parents gave the impression of wanting to keep as much as possible hidden in the well-intentioned hope of keeping their son in school.

He is the only child from a middle-class family. The home situation is good and orderly. According to the parents' information, he has developed normally in all aspects so far, without experiencing any major illnesses except for some childhood illnesses. There are no mental or nervous illnesses in the family.

Regarding his physical condition: A purely medical diagnosis could have been made during the initial outpatient examination. He exhibited a series of neurasthenic stigmata, which suggest abnormal excitability of the autonomic nervous system. He had a rather striking appearance with slightly wide eyelids that seemed to open wide, and his eyes had a distinct, dry brilliance. When things got lively in the clinic during a ball game between children, he immediately appeared very excited, his face turned bright red, and he looked heated and sweaty. He quickly entered a state of high excitement despite the unfamiliar environment. We will discuss the peculiarities of this excitability later.

The precise physical examination did not add much except for the fact of a high-level dermographism. However, the presence of particular emotional excitability combined with high vasomotor excitability allowed for the diagnosis of a neurasthenic condition. This diagnosis is essentially negative because it broadly designates some form of nervous state that does not conceal any serious physical or nervous illness, nor any pronounced mental illness, and can lead to extremely varied forms of educational difficulties. It also does not provide any indication for medical therapy. The term "neurasthenia" does not offer specific insights into therapeutic pedagogy or the nature of the child's psychological disorder that it designates. In this case, it was not possible to make decisions concerning his exclusion from school or other issues, such as how to continue his education, how best to care for him, whether to keep him at home or place him in an educational institution, based solely on this diagnosis. Therefore, his admission to the therapeutic pedagogy section was decided for further observation.

I will now present an excerpt from the comprehensive report summarizing the boy's stay in the section, which lasted approximately six weeks:

"In his overall behavior, he appears very childish and not very obedient. He is not accustomed to taking any orders into account. Only when reprimanded in a noticeable way does he seem surprised and puzzled, as if he were wondering what is wanted of him or why he is being bothered. If reprimanded for this reason, he responds with a flood of words, lots of shouting, and many gestures, but still, he is unable to finally listen or obey the requested order.

Authoritarian relationships with adults are entirely foreign to him: energy and punishments only succeed in irritating him, but any other approach challenges him to joke around and negotiate. One might think that a brief and objective manner of addressing things might have more success with him, but that is not the case either. Often, he is completely disconnected and behaves as if he were blind and deaf. At first, we thought it was a joke, especially when he ended up responding with a smile, giving the impression that he was making fun of us. The children perceived him like that each time and burst into mischievous laughter when he responded to a reprimand without suspecting anything. This stimulated him again, and he always had something else to say. Even a punishment (being isolated) meant nothing to him if he received such recognition from the other children. Only when he gets too bored with it does he come to ask for his punishment to be given back. Once again, he does so in a completely inappropriate manner, as if it were merely to fulfill a small innocent wish, but it's not quite the right time, so he must be more insistent. Again, we are surprised and irritated to find that the punishment and the unpleasant situation itself do not impress him at all. Thus, we are often quite helpless with him, feeling the desire to act even more energetically and yet recognizing that he is not capable of understanding the instructions and educational measures.

Similarly, the school situation, meaning proper learning, is not able to captivate him and place him in the general atmosphere and situation. For example, during written calculations, he speaks aloud; he must vocalize his horror at a failure, his anger at the difficulties of a task, and his triumph when he succeeds at something. This naturally earns him laughter from the others, and the teaching discipline is temporarily abandoned. The best solution is to place him alone somewhere and dictate a task to him. But it must be chosen so that he can accomplish it on his own; otherwise, he keeps pestering and asking for help because he can't do it alone. It's also useless to give him a chance to talk alone because if he senses even the slightest prospect of being heard, he turns to it with certainty and tenacity.

In general, if he wants something, it must be granted immediately. He never tires of monotonously demanding the same thing. He doesn't even consider a negative response. He also doesn't take into account that someone might be very busy; he insists like a small child on what he wants. He tries every means, running with each step, attempting to embrace and kiss the educator. There is no need for tenderness behind this behavior; rather, he lacks a sense of physical distance.

He doesn't have personal conflicts with others, and no interest binds him to his peers. But there are always disputes and scenes because of him. His loud and careless attitude unintentionally repels others, and during shared games, he irritates them because he always wants to talk and take his turn. This easily leads to quarrels that escalate into fights and blows. The other older boys regret the absence of camaraderie with him and, therefore, unite against him. Sometimes, they provoke him for their amusement. In excitement, he loses control, becomes red-faced like a turkey, and rages like a cat. A fight is certainly welcome, as any physical display pleases him, but his excitement renders him unable to face the others properly; he becomes blind and strikes, seemingly unaware of who the aggressor is or where they are. In this way, he pays a high price.

Sometimes, when he receives a stronger blow during a fight or bumps into something, he gets violently upset. Suddenly, one hears him pitifully crying from somewhere, as if something horrible had happened: "Help, help! Help me, I'm suffocating, I'm suffocating!" (when he once fell on his back). One rushes to the scene in horror and finds him lying there, his face bluish, gasping and unable to catch his breath. The only thing left to do is to talk to him and encourage him, waiting for the shock reaction to occur. For both children and adults, such a scene is always a very frightening and impressive experience because, for the moment, one believes that something terrible has happened. This happens not only during fights but also during chase games and ball games because in his excitement, he disregards the rules and spirit of the game, charging in at the wrong moment.

Despite the fact that he causes so much trouble, undermines discipline, and disrupts the children, no one can be angry with him; in fact, he is protected from the other children, even at the risk of their discontent. He himself bears no ill will toward the other children. Only when he cries and feels pain does he accuse them and justify himself, but as soon as he no longer feels the discomfort, he immediately becomes kind to them.

Now, let's try to draw conclusions from this account for our initial reflection on commanding and obeying. To do this, we will temporarily ignore medical and psychopathological knowledge and try to consider the problem of handling this difficult boy from the perspective of a naive educator, who does not intend to practice therapeutic pedagogy, but rather relies solely on their innate educational instinct and experiences acquired with healthy children. Such an educator is not prepared for exceptional and abnormal reactions. Their task is to bring this challenging boy into a group of children who are easy to educate."

Imagine one of these scenes as described in the report. It unfolds roughly as follows: among the children, for example during a break, there is a joyful and noisy atmosphere, everyone running around, making noise, and playfully engaging in some fighting. After a while, the educator arrives and demands silence and order so that teaching can resume. The other children easily fall silent upon the request, but he seems not to have heard and continues making noise. The previously calm atmosphere of the group is considerably disrupted by this. He is warned to "Stop!" and if he appears not to have heard, they shout a second time, this time loudly enough for him to hear. If that has no effect, the educator becomes forceful and talks to him as loud as possible, using threats. However, to their unpleasant and unexpected surprise, the boy behaves exactly as if he hadn't been told anything, continuing to make noise and be unruly.

This total and unusual lack of response to a measure that, based on experience, has always been effective in some way and is, in fact, an extreme last resort behind which there are only questionable pedagogical reserves, is always manifested in a very characteristic way in the educator, causing a subjective feeling of bewilderment and irritation. If the educator is naive, consciously aware of their authority, they don't understand such a lack of respect from the child, but only perceive it, as it appears to them, as a special insolence and impertinence. At least initially, they cannot think that this behavior might not be the consequence of the child's lack of respect for them, but rather an exceptional psychological state. Very regularly, in such cases, anger linked to a pulsional tendency towards aggression against the child arises. If they were to let go, they would have to fight or let their anger out in some other way. It is certain that, on such occasions, well before anyone might think it could be an abnormal state, parents regularly try to instill in their children the sense of authority they seem to lack by hitting them.

This violent and impulsive anger in situations where a child shows complete opposition or is absolutely resistant to an educational measure is strangely ingrained and difficult to suppress. One whose chosen profession is to deal with educational difficulties is not easily angered. The child's misbehavior is not an unexpected and unpleasant event for them but rather the sought-after problem that they have a mission to solve. When they find themselves facing the child in a live situation as an educator, they must play a special dual role, both concerning the child whom they must not only guide but also observe in their particularity and concerning themselves.

They must not only feel and act but also reflect on themselves, their actions, and reactions, in order to understand their correct and incorrect ways of interacting with the child. This unique relationship of the specialized educator with the child implies that they can at any moment face the child in an objective and composed manner. They also rely on this and become accustomed to objectifying their anger immediately if it arises, using it as a symptom. It has been found that assuming such a highly objectified attitude, the educator's anger itself indicates a severe psychological abnormality in the child. At the time, Lazar drew attention to this phenomenon in oral communications and lectures, a phenomenon he first noticed in his work as a juvenile judge. He reported that he could regularly conclude that a serious psychological abnormality was present and that he was always right when a young person behaved so outrageously before the judge that it angered him.

In the scene described above, the educator's anger is due to an erroneous emotional evaluation of the boy's reaction. His behavior is considered particularly severe disobedience, which makes the educator angry. This mistaken judgment also results in an erroneous pedagogical attitude, as the usual procedure for dealing with disobedience proves futile and ineffective. It turns out that in this situation, reprimands and punishments are in vain because they do not reach the boy. One would want to punish him in an exemplary manner, if only because of the other children who see him as nothing other than disobedient and insolent, and unexpectedly, they are faced with a boy who expresses the feeling of his innocence with the seal of honesty and conviction. In practice, the problem is further exacerbated because the usual educational approach leads to new exhausting struggles between the educator and the child. Once the initial moment of perplexity has passed, the educator will have to find another effective educational method for this child in future situations.

One thing is particularly striking: this extraordinary behavior does not make him lose the sympathy of his educators, even though it makes their lives so difficult. He is well-liked, and rightly so, as he is kind and obedient by nature. There are also enough situations in which he behaves very well, follows the rules perfectly, and is completely docile. His actions are generally devoid of any trace of malice or intentional malevolence. All of this would not make sense if this apparent insolence and stubbornness stemmed from malice or primary insensitivity.

The key to the problem lies in the question of what occasions or conditions lead him not to listen at all. Upon examining this question, one quickly arrives at the conclusion that he is truly closed off to his surroundings and is unable to appropriate anything when he becomes more intensely focused on an object with fervor. He immediately enters a state of intense excitement in which the rest of the world no longer exists for him. Not hearing the order is just part of this error, which also manifests itself in the most diverse occasions. Every game leads to such excitement, in which he shows no consideration for his peers, no concern for his own safety, and no respect for the rules of the game. In his enthusiasm, he may completely forget that there are still people around him. It can happen that, in such a situation, he reflexively pushes away the adult who wants to stop him or say something to him, as if the adult were just an object. In the state of anger, he is the least influenced. Only through brute force can he be restrained from embarking on a blind race.

He is particularly excitable. Only in entirely indifferent situations, for example, in a perfectly objective and impersonal conversation, can one get to know him as a calm, polite, and rather intelligent person. Everything that, in other children, is merely sentimental, manifests in him as affect with accompanying signs of excitement. The smallest and most trivial everyday occasions, joys, expectations, desires, interests, physical pains, fears—everything leads to exaggerated consequences. In this state of excitement, the horizon of his consciousness is greatly narrowed in the exclusive direction of the intentional object of the dominating affect. As a result, any new influence, such as an order, cannot take effect. He is unable to process the order that reaches his ears, so, in the state of excitement, he behaves as if he were not able to hear.

Once we understand the mechanism of his failure correctly, our emotional attitude changes, and we are already freed from the anger reaction described earlier. We can now behave much more freely and appropriately towards him. Efforts will be made to organize his life in a way that minimizes exciting stimuli. But when he is in an excited state, during which there is no active control of affect or introspection, one must, without getting angry, protect both his surroundings and him from his own reckless actions using appropriate means. His outbursts of affect have no lasting effect, and they no longer carry emotional weight in memory; hence, they are quickly forgotten. Therefore, it only makes sense to deal with the present. Trying to teach him how to avoid such discomfort in the future would be a futile endeavor.

We talked at the beginning about how a child cannot understand an order to which the correct emotional emphasis is not given through corresponding means of expression. In the example of the five-year-old boy, this went so far that the child did not even hear what the educator was saying to him. This is also true of the last child we mentioned. However, the mechanism of disturbance is fundamentally different in both cases. In one case, it was due to a faulty order; in the second case, a correct form of the order was assumed. The mistake was then attributed to the child who, under certain circumstances, especially in a state of excitement, was so completely isolated from his environment that the order could not reach him.

But the mechanism of disturbance we have just described does not yet fully explain his strange behavior towards the educator, as described in the behavioral report. There is still a defect that partly reinforces the first one but also acts partly independently.

Even if a relationship has been established between him and the educator, he often behaves very unpleasantly and irritatingly. For example: he has misbehaved again, the educator has laboriously put him in a receptive state and is reprimanding him energetically. At that moment, the educator expects the boy to respond accordingly to the reprimand, to show embarrassment or to let the unpleasant event pass without saying anything, to defend himself, to cry, or to do whatever a child would normally do in such a situation, depending on his feelings or temperament. But instead, there is something completely different, unexpected, and inappropriate. He might respond to the reprimands with a stupid joke or, if approached indignantly, answer in a conversational tone or say "yes, yes" in passing and turn to something else.

When a sudden, more severe educational measure is followed by such a response, from which it can be inferred that the measure leaves him indifferent or that he even seems to mock it, it has an almost more unpleasant effect on the educator than the total ignorance of an order described initially. Such insensitivity to reprimands and punishments is considered, according to common ethical criteria, as insensitivity or brutality. As one is not able to act upon the child, they suddenly feel powerless and helpless, and they revert to the particular reaction of irritation and anger that we have already discussed in detail above.

As we get to know him, we stop believing in his malice. His error lies in an entirely different domain than that of character or morals. This is precisely what constitutes the essential part of the influence that the adult's personality has on the child, which makes no impression on him. He cannot scold or threaten him because, in a certain way, it has no effect, even if he hears it in a receptive phase. But he also does not sense the look by which someone wants to communicate something to him; he does not sense whether someone behaves negatively towards him or is kindly disposed towards him, showing interest and concern. In short, he never knows what feelings and moods dominate his educator at any given moment and are expressed towards him not only through words but also through gestures, facial expressions, and the emphasis of words. As a result, misunderstandings always arise. Since he does not grasp the emotional content of the address, his responses and reactive actions are also incorrect. He takes something entirely serious as a joke and responds with a joke, he considers an indifferent word as a threat due to its emphasis, and thus, he does not pay attention to it. He is given an urgent task, and he refuses it as if the person asking were an accomplice to whom he has neither the desire nor the reason to please. He does not sense the atmosphere of the group of children around him, so he cannot adapt to it and appears everywhere as an alien and disruptive presence. That is why he is unusable when discipline, team spirit, cooperation during gymnastics, boys' games, or any other communal activity is required; that is also why he is not able to learn the necessary behavior at school.

Overall, these two problems, his particular excitability with its psychic barrier and the lack of understanding of the emotional content of speech, must intertwine and amplify each other. His inappropriate behavior constantly causes conflicts, leading to excitement in which he becomes exalted without measure. And if he is particularly blind and deaf in this excitement, it is certainly partly because what is said to him affects him in a completely different and weakened way compared to other people, as the emotional emphasis of the speech addressed to him, which is not negligible at such moments, goes unnoticed by him.

As a result, significant educational difficulties arise, which made him remarkable among so many difficult children, even in the station of remedial education, and probably even more so in secondary school, where he cannot be accommodated or taken into consideration. Given his high excitability, it seems credible that he is much calmer at home, where the environment is much quieter than at school and where there is much less excitement. For this reason, parents have been advised to homeschool him. It has been more than six months since then, and everything is going well at home, revealing that, in private, he is not as difficult to teach, and he learns quite well.

PART II

In the first part of this work, we attempted, during the analysis of a case, to consider educational difficulties from a diagnostic perspective—meaning not as a medical or psychiatric problem, but as an educational problem. To reach this position, we deliberately moved away from any scientifically established symptomatic scheme and ultimately relied on the experiences of the observing educator. Such an approach is justified by the field of special education itself, which is not meant to diagnose medical issues in pediatrics or psychiatry but to examine and address educational difficulties. However, this doesn't mean that pediatric or psychiatric approaches are rejected; rather, they are intrinsically connected to remedial education as a science, providing inspiration to it. But an exclusively pediatric approach can only answer questions regarding physical health or illness, and an exclusively psychiatric approach can only address the nature and degree of mental disorders. Alone, neither can solve educational problems.

A differential diagnosis in remedial education would be needed, taking the most original manifestation of various educational difficulties as a starting point, as experienced by the observer or educator, somewhat like an original symptom. This diagnosis should describe their aspects, as well as the different causes that might provoke them, along with their distinctive characteristics. Moreover, it should indicate the appropriate curative treatment based on the cause.

Such an original symptom of remedial education is this

unexpected and strangely incorrect reaction of a child to an order. This reaction is regularly accompanied by the educator's subjective feelings of surprise, irritation, powerlessness, or anger. Those who deal extensively with challenging individuals often encounter this symptom. It always indicates that the child did not understand or misinterpreted the given order. The educator's feeling of irritation indicates that they have not yet correctly assessed the child's particular mode of reaction. It is also justified to conclude that the educator did not behave pedagogically correctly towards the child and that a different approach is needed than what was used previously.

Such abnormal misunderstanding of orders and its resulting consequences can have various psychopathological origins. Connecting and analyzing these origins are of crucial practical importance for the educator, as each of them demands a different educational and therapeutic approach. We will now attempt to classify them into different groups and subgroups according to these causes and indicate the resulting images in their most significant moments. We will outline, as an example, a chapter of such a utopian differential diagnosis as we envision it.

A. The first group includes all children who appear to disobey because, in certain circumstances, they are incapable of anticipating the given orders. This group is characterized by the fact that the child reacts to the order as if it had not been given. In anamnestic reports, it is typically said, "...as if they didn't hear," which implicitly suggests that the apprehension of the order was assumed.

1) The most extreme example is the fairly common cases of undiagnosed deafness in very young children.

The diagnosis of deafness is often made very late by parents and sometimes by doctors, in intellectually complete children, mistakenly assuming it to be laziness in speaking or a late start in speech development. The oldest case of this kind that I know of dates back to the age of 6. Even at that time, the parents refused to believe the facts, and a doctor diagnosed it as a vague psychic inhibition of speech. In these cases, people are often deceived by the fact that some remnants of hearing can be detected. For example, the children may express joy when listening to music, playing the radio or gramophone, or reacting to everyday or exam room noises. Often, the sensitivity of all these children to subtle vibrations accompanying loud noises is also interpreted as auditory ability.

With all deaf children, an excellent understanding of gestures and facial expressions of the deaf child develops very early, when there is a beginning of communication. This allows for a simulated understanding of language. If, as is inevitable, such a child fails sometimes—either because they cannot see the person giving the order and therefore cannot read the instruction, or because the order goes beyond the limits of their gestural comprehension—the described image above results. From the adult's perspective, this appears as gratuitous disobedience, marked by a certain stubbornness since the error is repeated constantly despite energetic countermeasures, making the child, in the eyes of the unsuspecting adult, appear headstrong and impressionable when the same order is repeated.

If such misunderstandings repeat with resulting conflicts, children are constantly subjected to pressures of faults they are helpless to understand. As a secondary development, a habitual attitude of opposition or negativism towards adults can emerge (see Group C). The overall educational situation is further aggravated.

The correct diagnosis then enables not only the appropriate therapy for artistic teaching of reading and speech, but it also prompts a complete change in the educator's attitude. The child's insubordinate behavior in many past instances of anger suddenly becomes understandable; the educator realizes that the child couldn't even know what was expected of them and why they were being punished. The educator's relationship with the child is automatically altered. Previously, they tried to encourage or force the child to speak and felt it necessary to speak to them as much as possible. Now, this is unnecessary, and it is replaced by a more appropriate reinforcement of verbal expression through gestures and facial expressions, which the adult systematically uses when faced with a deaf child. This provides better possibilities for communication and understanding, and the child can be better supported in their intellectual development.

Moreover, the educational situation is fundamentally different. As children are no longer constantly burdened with innocent sins, their relationship with the educator improves and becomes less laden with conflicts and misunderstandings. Once the diagnosis is established, the children regularly become freer and more confident.

2) The educational image of such irritating and seemingly unmotivated disobedience can also be simulated by unrecognized absences, if they occur frequently enough.

For example, the teacher may call a child during such an absent moment, and they do not react at all. Or in gymnastics, the child suddenly disobeys an order for no apparent reason, even though they participated entirely correctly before, and remains standing, rigid, and frozen. This is extremely perplexing when the correct diagnosis is unknown, and there is a temptation to make erroneous interpretations. The most frequent assumptions are inattention or disobedience. Sometimes, such children have been brought to us because their acts were wrongly thought to be indecent acts of masturbation. Apparently, the fixed gaze and the change in color in these children were interpreted as an orgasm. The correct diagnosis is often not easy to establish in these cases because, in addition to the absences, these children often exhibit other behavioral anomalies that make the picture confusing. It is a fortunate coincidence if, during the brief observation time in a morning ambulance, someone sees such an equivalent who can also recognize it.

3) Here, we must include the important and variable group of neuropathic children, in whom various attentional behavior disorders lead to apparent disobedience. In principle, two types of disorders can be distinguished in this category:

a) The first is characterized by the fact that the direction of attention is currently so completely fixed on a specific intentional object that the normal psychic mobility and distractibility, which otherwise exist, are canceled out or made very difficult. This occurs in the many affective and excitation states, extremely variable in form and coloration, which are frequently encountered in neuropathic children. In these states of excitement, consciousness is so completely filled with an object, for example, that of anger, desire, or interest, that the normal movement allowing an individual to see a different object in each glance disappears. There is no other object in the center of their mental visual field. The comparison with blinkers or with a visual field limited to central vision illustrates what we mean. What is happening, so to speak, at the periphery of the spiritual visual field certainly strikes the external senses, but the central consciousness does not adapt to it, even with the greatest intensity of stimulation.

b) Curiously, the same practical effect can occur when a fixation of attention on a specific object is not possible at a given moment, as is the case in extreme cases of "absent-mindedness" or "daydreaming." One cannot speak here of attention in the usual sense of the term, which grasps an object, places it in the center of the mind, and elevates it to full conscious clarity. Whatever is happening in the individual at such a moment is not determinable; in any case, they seem closed to stimuli from the outside world. States of excitement as well as states of joylessness can also occasionally occur in a normal child. It would be logical to assume that the corresponding pathological states are merely a quantitative increase of physiological reaction modes. The fact that such attention disorders also occur in the normal subject is confirmed by the many common expressions we have to describe them: a person is described as absent-minded, inattentive, absorbed, or engrossed in work, blind with anger, oblivious to pain, or mad with joy, etc. However, neuropathic states differ from these physiological states precisely in the fact that the restriction of attention is particularly strong. It is precisely the discrepancy between the perhaps not so high excitement or oblivion and the complete closure of the child that is particularly striking here. A child looks ahead, empty; one might think that a warning shout could more easily wake them up. But, to the great surprise of the educator, they behave as if they were blind and deaf and can only be brought back to the present through vigorous interventions. Another child runs around enjoying their motor skills; it is not difficult to stop this usually docile child, and one is astonished to find that it can only be achieved by brute force. Such situations have already been described in the first, albeit very complex, case, but two others will follow to illustrate what has been said:

Case 2: Johann M., 8 years, 11 months (excerpt from the anamnesis).

He was brought in by his stepmother due to bad behavior at school and at home.

He completed his third year of primary school and is a good student, but he behaves very badly at school. It's so severe that he had to be excluded from gymnastics classes and all class excursions.

He hits, pinches, bites, and twists other children's fingers. There is a fear that he might seriously injure someone someday. He has already kicked a girl in the stomach and bitten another on the throat.

He is also very disruptive in class. He fools around with other children, does not pay attention, is dreamy, and never listens to the teacher at first glance;

he usually starts working only after others have finished.

At home, he is also very difficult, rebellious, and non-compliant. He does not get along with his brothers and sisters, accuses them, and slanders them. But there are days when he behaves very well. Sometimes, he can sit for hours looking ahead. Suddenly, he starts jumping and getting wild.

He is negligent and needs to be reminded to go to the bathroom, brush his teeth, or use the toilet. Occasionally, he wets the bed at night. The stepmother also reports sexual escapades with a girl, allegedly in public, in a park. He also once incited his stepsister to play games in bed.

The father is 47 years old, a railway worker, and a quarrelsome man. There are frequent disputes at home. Last year, a complaint was filed against him for mistreating the boy.

The mother died of tuberculosis a few years ago. The stepmother has been with the boys for two years. She also gives an impression of irritation and nervousness.

Regarding his somatic condition: the boy is much too tall for his age, and he also looks much older; one could estimate him to be around ten or eleven years old. He has an asthenic physique. This impression of asthenia is further reinforced by his slumped posture; he always stands and sits with his arms hanging down. The general hypotonia is also evident in his vacant, limp, and unexpressive face, with his mouth usually open. Even when excited, his face does not animate, and only the redness and the rising glow of his eyes give away his emotions. His internal organs are normal. Hearing is normal. Intelligence is average.

The report on his behavior after several weeks of observation in the service is as follows:

"From the first day, he has been undisciplined, often disobedient, runs

around and rushes, makes stupid jokes, and plays pranks. In this state, he does not listen to warnings at all; we actually thought for a while that he might be deaf. But then, he should also be blind since he does not react to a fixed gaze either; he is completely disconnected from the situation. Sometimes, he sits with an expressive face, staring into space, and does not respond when called. Initially, we were outraged by this lack of responsiveness. If we are firm in trying to make him understand that he needs to be reprimanded, he laughs at us, partly out of embarrassment and partly because he is surprised at such energetic actions against him."

"It's as if he has his own gestures, as if he is connected to a process, and he only occasionally engages with the situation when it is in sync with him. When pressed, he seems angry and unable to shake off his excesses."

"During gymnastics, he is generally unbearable; either he does not hear the orders, or he continues doing gymnastics when we have already taken a break. He takes advantage of every moment of inattention to slide on the floor and shake himself. He also disrupts group games. During study time, when the situation is calmer, he does better. He is calm and persevering when working alone. He also resists drawing. In general, he is much easier to handle alone than in a group, as he is calmer when the numerous stimuli of the noisy and agitated crowd disappear."

Case 3: Johann B., 7 years, 10 months (excerpt from the anamnesis).

His mother brings him on orders from the youth office due to serious educational difficulties at school and at home.

Until the age of four, he was very well-behaved. Then he went to a public kindergarten where, from the beginning, there were complaints because he did not follow and was wild and brutal with other children. Similar complaints are now coming from the school. He has completed the first grade and is an excellent student, with only "A" grades on his school report, including behavior (?), except for a "B" in writing. But he is very bad; he cannot sit quietly, does not pay attention, and does not fit into the class discipline.

Since starting school, he has also been very difficult at home. He cannot play quietly with his brothers and sisters; either he fights with them and shakes them, or he withdraws and plays alone. He prefers monotonous technical games.

He is never truly sad or joyful; either he is dreamy or gets agitated. Often, he sits with vacant eyes or speaks and gesticulates vigorously for himself.

He often walks alone on the street, stops when he sees or hears something, and forgets everything else. If sent to run errands, he does not return home for hours, and he spends the money he took. Or he hides his school bag behind the house gate after school and runs away, returning two or three hours later. He was enrolled in a day center to be supervised continuously, but he only attended regularly for a short period and then kept away.

At home, he took small amounts of money and food, and he also stole fruits while passing by stores. At the day center, he took clothing.

The father, aged 32, is described by the mother as very selfish and living withdrawn. He is a cobbler's assistant and very conscientious in his work. He has 12 siblings, all of whom are said to be carefree. Many of them have had trouble with the police for minor thefts. The mother, aged 27, claims to have lung problems.

There are two other children, a four-year-old brother and a two-year-old sibling.

Regarding his somatic condition: He is too small for his age, with senile features on his face, looking poor. He has few facial expressions. When afraid or excited, he becomes very red and sweats a lot.

Rachitic skeleton, mild hydrocephalus, funnel chest. Muscles are very weak but well-toned. Tonus is rather reduced. Neurologically normal. No dermographism. Very good intelligence.

Here is an excerpt from the observation report in the service:

"Among the children, when the atmosphere is a bit joyful, he becomes particularly violent. He does not notice calls, threats, or even touches; we have to exclude him from the group, only then does he come back to himself. It cannot be called disobedience because he does not have control over himself. He almost reflexively reacts to a joyful mood and cannot hold back. If we reprimand him for his inappropriate behavior, he becomes very offended. It seems he does not realize how badly he behaved."

"During play, he always looks red, messy, and sweaty."

"In an individual conversation or learning session, he is initially inhibited, but then becomes talkative, gives mature answers, and appears older than he is. In this situation, he gives the impression of being quite pleasant and intelligent."

These two cases represent a relatively common type of dissociation in school-age children. We have chosen to present it in more detail among the many and varied neuropathic symptoms because it is precisely in these cases that the psychopathological phenomena in question are elaborated in a particularly pure manner.

What characterizes both cases is first the state of particular excitement. Lazar used to describe it very concisely as "the mood of children." At the end of children's parties, a similar, difficult-to-influence excitement also settles in many healthy children, an extreme increase in exuberant mood that often ends sadly with a thunderstorm or punishment.

In this state, the physical signs of excitement, strong vasomotor and vegetative reactions, are particularly pronounced. Thus, the children take on this characteristic appearance, mentioned several times before, immediately after the onset of excitement. Their faces become bright red, they sweat a lot, and their eyes shine with excitement. They are seized with frenzy and agitation that gives the impression of something physically urgent. Sometimes, they give in to their urge to move by running senselessly, jumping, and screaming. Alternatively, they engage in more serious acts, fights, games, aggression against other children, or other reprehensible acts. It is always clear that it is not just what they do that is essential but mostly that they move, expend energy, and heed the strong motor impulses.

These neuropathic children are most often seen agitated in the evening. However, this can also be triggered at any time of the day if the cause is found. Anything stimulating in the environment can act as a triggering factor, a burst of gaiety or noise, a lively movement, or amusing confusion among the surrounding children. Any transition from disciplined calm to unsupervised freedom can provoke this agitation. Therefore, these children often complain of feeling uncomfortable during breaks, on the way back from school, in the park, and generally when playing freely with other children.

It is noise, movement, and agitation itself that provoke the excitement, even if the primary cause of the mood change in the environment remains hidden from the children. They do not really experience the mood of the environment but are merely brought into a state of excitement by the processes - almost automatically. The course of this excitement is also strangely independent of the general uniform mood of the surrounding children. The general merriment, which you seem to have witnessed, followed its normal course; it increased, reached its peak, and subsided.

But the agitation of this child, once triggered, continued unchanged throughout that time and persists with the same intensity, even though everyone else has been silent for a long time. Only at the moment of the explosion and climax of the general mood can he give the impression of vibrating at the same rhythm as the others, but otherwise, in his agitation, he appears unsuitable and disruptive, like an alien body within the group of children.

Moreover, it turns out that, in this state, the child is not influenceable; he is deaf to admonitions, orders, reminders, and prohibitions, as he is completely closed off to his environment and does not see or hear what is happening around him.

In these same neuropathic children who easily fall into a frenzied excitement, we can very often observe another state of consciousness, which seems to be polar opposite to the first. Indeed, we can often see them dreamy and lost. Even in this state, they feel detached from their environment and incapable of receiving orders. They sit and stare into space or are engrossed in any place. At school, this loss resembles a particular inattention; they do not collaborate, tinker around, and are not ready to respond when called; they never know what tasks have been assigned to them.

If they have to work alone, they never finish because they keep losing focus. This loss is also evident when they walk alone on the street. They drift while daydreaming, on the one hand, not seeing or hearing what is happening around them and being closed off to the people they pass, and on the other hand, drawn and captivated by many things. If you observe them, you can see an uninterrupted alternation of impulses and instinctive actions. They are at the mercy of whatever attracts them. It is only surprising that nothing happens to them and that they eventually return home, even with hours of delay. It is easy to understand that, in the absence of increased supervision, they readily give in to negligence on the street or even engage in criminal acts.

Children are by no means constantly caught in excitement or in oblivion. There is also a state of free present attention for them. It is often surprising to see how intelligent, thoughtful, and well-adjusted they can be. They seem out of step with their usual behavior. They are particularly well-disposed when under the direct influence of an adult, during a conversation, or when someone takes care of them or plays with them. The influence of an adult helps them stay awake and calm. This is why they perform tasks well and quickly under continuous adult supervision, even if they are not materially helped, but they take an infinite amount of time to complete them, get dirty, and make mistakes when they have to work alone. This happens if they are constantly being reminded, while they lose themselves if left to their own devices. But the adult is always ready to draw the conclusion from this conditional capacity: "He can if he wants."

It is important to emphasize that these two cases are just paradigms of a set of symptoms quite common in curative pedagogy, which, according to the usual diagnosis, should be classified within the circle of neuropathic symptoms. In the case of a similar attentional behavior disorder, the resulting images of dyssociality can be extremely variable, depending on the quality of the underlying disorder itself, its combination with other disorders, such as those of intelligence, instinctive or emotional sphere, and also depending on the child's other nature and character and their aptitude for life.

B. In the first group of abnormal disobedience, all cases where the child, for one reason or another, is not at all able to understand the order, have been included. In a second group, we find all cases where the child receives the order and comprehends it from a logical and material point of view. But for the emotional content of the order, for what is not expressed in words, the child lacks the receiving organ. Hence, the response reaction must be incorrect. Such a child hears the words "Come here" and objectively understands that the educator has given them the order to go to them. But they do not understand what it means or what intention might lie behind the request. The educator might call them once to give an order, another time to ask them a favor, a third time to fix something on their clothes, then to punish them or to joke with them, to say something encouraging, etc. For a normal child, the way they are called reveals a lot of these intentions. They must then act accordingly; they will be frightened or embarrassed if they see the educator angry, they will follow with indifference if it is an indifferent matter, they will gladly respond to a friendly call, they will notice a joke and be careful not to fall for it.

All of this, a child cannot do if they do not have a rough idea of what the educator wants from them. This becomes most clearly evident and least pleasant when the child does not take a very serious, energetic, or urgent order seriously and thus reacts as if it were not important and as if they were free to carry it out or not. They do not comply, start talking, or try to push the matter aside with a joke or a valid remark. What is characteristic is not so much the fact that they do not comply but rather that the response is entirely inappropriate to the order given. For example, if they are seriously appealed to their sense of honor, the child responds with laughter and boldness that would be permissible at most in a game. If one does not know that this mistaken reaction comes from a misunderstanding of the situation, then one must take it as insolence.

The pedagogical consequences of such a mistaken order-taking, with its unpleasant and irritating misunderstandings, have already been described in case 1. It has been demonstrated that this error - and not only in this case, but generally - is part of a broader disorder. All these children lack an intuitive understanding of the living situation they are in.

This lack of understanding of the situation is most clearly manifested as one of the characteristic manifestations of what psychiatrists refer to as an "epileptic character." But it is by no means limited to epileptoid psychopathy. The "troublesome," "clingy," "distant" behavior of epileptics is only a consequence of such a misunderstanding of the situation and not the only one. But it is the most evident to someone who only encounters epileptics intermittently, as is the case, for example, with a doctor who only makes regular visits or has consultations with the patient. By constantly being in their company, especially with other children, one perceives this disorder not only as annoying behavior but also as a dissociability and difficulty in education. In a way, these children are always outside the mass of others, as soon as they are dominated by a common spirit. They cannot feel a collective mood or emotion, a common interest, a common will, to the extent that they cannot express it in words. This is why they always disturb the community by being different from others, making noise at the wrong time, getting into fights, being funny, making jokes. They cannot take into account the desires and feelings of their peers; they bother educators with their remarks, wishes, and complaints at the wrong time. Moreover, their lack of tact easily leads them into conflicts, exacerbated by their frequent irritability, and the fact that their opponents always think they are wrong without realizing how much they have disturbed them.

These children with epileptoid contact disorders are all remarkably uncritical and unconcerned about the position they occupy in the surrounding society. Either the other children do not consider them as full-fledged beings, given their peculiarities if the disorder is so pronounced that even naive children are impressed by it as an anomaly. Or, if not, they are treated with hostility because they show themselves uncooperative. The educator is also forced to treat them differently from others; they must isolate them if they disturb too much, constantly remind them of the rules, shake them if they become too insistent. Faced with such treatment, anyone with even a little sensitivity would eventually become shy, fearful, bitter, or malicious and withdraw if possible from society. But these children get angry if another child mistreats them, they cry if something unpleasant happens to them from the educator. But on a personal level, they are not affected, they are never long offended or hurt, the memory of what they have suffered is not etched into their memory, and they do not harbor bitterness. They also do not feel that something is wrong with them; they never feel uncertain or helpless in the many situations they dislike. Similarly, they never learn to avoid situations where they feel so bad; they do not think about withdrawing from children or being arrogant towards the educator. Despite all the bad experiences, the same conflicts occur, they encounter the same inconveniences, they make the same mistakes.

C. 1. Other forms of dissociation and disobedience appear when children feel that something is wrong with them, when they feel uncertain and powerless in the face of demands, or when they are constantly irritated by the rejection behavior of their surroundings or frequent disciplinary sanctions. Depending on the nature of the child, different habitual attitudes of defense and opposition develop. The prerequisite is the endogenous factor of a certain hypersensitivity. If this is present, various errors and weaknesses of the child can lead to such defense reactions.

Case 4 - Fritz M., 4 years and 2 months old (excerpt from the anamnesis).

The child is sent with his mother by the youth office. The mother wants to send him to kindergarten, but the kindergarten refuses to keep him because he is particularly mischievous, does not follow the educator's instructions, attacks her, and tries to hit her, and he is also aggressive towards other children. They ask what to do with the child because the mother cannot handle him either.

The mother recounts that he was very well-behaved until the age of 4. Then, he started going to kindergarten, and at the beginning, everything was fine, but the mentioned complaints began quickly. At home as well, he became increasingly mischievous. He behaves very badly, especially with his mother; he tries to hit her in anger and tear her clothes. He also goes after his younger brother, sometimes using very dangerous objects.

The early anamnesis reveals that he only learned to walk at the age of 19 months and started speaking at the age of 3.

Regarding his physical condition: He is a robust boy in good physical health. He strikingly resembles his two older siblings. The contrast between his dark eyes and light blond hair is remarkable. However, his face is much less differentiated than that of his siblings; his facial features are notably coarser. Additionally, the shape of his skull is pathologically deformed, showing turricéphalie.

Apart from that, there are no pathologies present, no signs of neurological disorders, and no neuropathic stigmas.

The final result of the intelligence examination is: debility, primitive practical usefulness, and weak personal contact. Here is an excerpt from the observation report of the service:

"An incomprehensible boy. Always an unexpected reaction. He responds insolently to kindness, yells, insults, and hits in the face. He disregards reprimands and continues to do what is prohibited. For example, if he is sent

away from one place, he diligently returns from the other side until one must become forceful and warn him. But even then, he reacts to anger by sticking out his tongue as much as he can, making a long nose, or dramatically repeating a quote from an idol. Threatening or forbidding only worsens the situation. Even if brought back to his place and reproached, he immediately returns to his previous behavior, grossly insulting and sticking out his tongue to idolize or dishonor the other children. Words are of no use. The best way to calm him down is to remove him from punishment in silence and put him back in his place."

"Suddenly, even if there was a scene before, he can start chatting and making up stories with a serious expression. He cannot look at faces; he becomes embarrassed if he suddenly feels someone's gaze on him and looks down or covers his face with his hand."

"He doesn't understand any form of concession. He only responds to a request when it concerns something daily and concrete. Otherwise, when something is asked of him, it is always better to take him by the hand and lead him without speaking."

"He can talk to himself, talking to himself, answering his own questions. If another child bothers him, he gets very angry, clenches his teeth, and immediately hits. He doesn't really know how to play and doesn't recognize toys either. During naptime or in the evening when everything is already calm, he makes noise without caring about his surroundings; no threat is useful, he always starts again."

In this case as well, the cause of his failure is evidently a poor understanding or misunderstanding of commands. It is likely that due to his reduced intellectual abilities, he doesn't grasp many of the educator's requirements, even on a basic level. However, there are plenty of mentally challenged individuals who have an excellent rapport with their educators, even in cases of severe language comprehension issues. Even if they don't fully understand the words, they can often sense with great certainty what is being asked and how it is understood, and then adeptly adjust their behavior accordingly. This intuitive understanding of the situation is lacking in him, which results in his slow reactions to different educational measures.

It is important to note that the form of these reactions is very different in him compared to all those we have discussed previously. The other children always disobeyed without realizing it, and the numerous misunderstandings and conflicts hardly disturbed their psychological balance. However, in the case of the last boy described, according to the report, we can no longer speak of unintentional misbehavior because when addressed by an adult with any demand, he almost consistently reacts aggressively, visibly and consciously refusing to obey or intentionally doing the opposite of what is asked. In such situations, he is not careless at all; on the contrary, along with his lack of understanding of the situation, there is a primary hypersensitivity, whether it's about his own inadequacy or the lack of kindness from others. He is constantly under pressure, feeling uneasy and unsure of himself due to his frequent negative experiences in certain critical situations for him. He feels helpless, expecting punishment and yet unsure of how to do better. This insecurity and fear of an inevitable conflict then lead to surprising aggressive acts; in his irritation, he responds to the anticipated discomfort with a furious attack or refusal to obey. This triggers further repressions from the educator, worsening the child's situation. The conflicts escalate more and more, and the child's aggressive behavior becomes habitual over time, automatically triggered in appropriate situations.

The interplay of three original elements plays a decisive role in the emergence of this dissociability:

1. Primary hypersensitivity,

2. Some weakness or defect in the child on which sensitivity can focus (in case 4, the mental impairment and lack of understanding of the situation),

3. The exogenous moment of the educator's wrong attitude, who does not comprehend the child's sensitivity and thus cannot accommodate their mistakes and weaknesses.

The greater the child's sensitivity, the smaller and more insignificant the weakness and error in the educator's attitude can be. In the end, it may only involve minor misunderstandings, where the educator's behaviors and expressions are constantly misinterpreted by the child as rejection, coldness, or reproach, or conversely, when the educator misinterprets the child's reactions, causing minor injustices. In particularly sensitive or dependent children, this can already trigger significant dissociability.

These forms of dissociability based on paranoid psychopathy are most frequently observed in boys over 10 years old and adolescents. A deeper analysis reveals that in these cases, there is an underlying weakness in the individual, which is affected by hypersensitivity. Based on our experiences, these are often boys whose learning disabilities or lack of intelligence starkly contrast with the position they hold in their environment, a position that would be expected to match their nature. They often stand out in appearance, presentation, and behavior, attempting to assert a position they are not capable of maintaining. Given the impression their personality gives in the world, one would expect various intellectual qualities from them, and thus it comes as a surprise when intelligence tests and examination of their academic performance yield very mediocre or below-average results.

In other cases, such dissociability may conceal more serious disorders. Children rebel and refuse to obey precisely where they sense that what is demanded of them exceeds the limits of their abilities.

This is the case, for example, with children suffering from language disorders or language development delays when they are asked to make specific efforts to speak, or with intellectually inferior children. The primary flaws are often completely masked by dissociability. One must always consider these possibilities, especially with mute children or those who refuse to attend school. Such oppositional or negativistic traits can also develop in unrecognized deaf-mute children (Group A, 1).

All these cases are particularly receptive to educational therapy if, preferably in a new environment, their sensitivity and other weaknesses are accommodated. Once the excitement aspect dissipates from their lives and their good qualities can be highlighted, calmness gradually sets in, and the rebellion fades away. In light of this surprising success, one might be tempted to make a particularly favorable prognosis and consider dissociability as exclusively exogenous. However, it is regularly observed that these children and adolescents always behave impeccably in the gentle atmosphere of an institution, but very often, their previous difficulties reemerge when they are confronted with the inevitable challenges of ordinary life after their release.

These hypersensitive individuals are indeed the ones for whom encouragement therapy is most appropriate. However, expecting an educator to encourage and treat with kindness an angry, grumbling, or recalcitrant child is certainly easier said than done. The educator cannot feign a friendly attitude in the long run if they are inwardly angry, perplexed, or despairing due to the child's behavior. Likewise, a critical and arbitrary attitude can, at best, have a spoiling effect or, because it is unnatural, repel the child. In such cases, general parenting advice is of little use if it only indicates how to behave with the child. Given the child's behavior, it seems impossible, without explanation, to be genuinely kind to him; it is unclear how this strange, paradoxical, and sentimental advice could be successful, so it is rarely followed. Moreover, according to our experience, it is incorrect because it is not an insistent behavior but a behavior as impersonal as possible that is appropriate in these cases. The child must only feel respected and appreciated for their true worth. Here too, it is necessary to change the educator's opinion of the child above all else. If one can make the educator understand the child's character and thus the causes of their provocative behavior, explain their weaknesses, and highlight their abilities and qualities, it automatically leads to a correction of the educational approach. However, to achieve this, one must make an effort to seek and find the child's weaknesses and qualities.

2) Next, we will discuss another form of paradoxical refusal to obey, which also has an underlying hypersensitivity. The

dyssociality that develops from it most often appears in the form of negativism, obsessive disobedience, or refusal. The sensitivity underlying this negativism is somewhat different from the one we just talked about. Both are often found together, for example, in case 4, but negativism frequently appears alone, creating a distinct and descriptive symptomatic picture.

It should be noted that many of these highly sensitive children also react to kindness with refusal, especially when the kindness is strongly imposed and cannot be misinterpreted, such as in the case of certain affectionate and insistent reprimands, physical gestures like caresses, pats, hugs, specific compliments, or flattery.

In the most severe cases, they become irritated by any intense personal address directed at them, as well as any expressive gaze directed towards them, which they try to avoid. In the report on case 4, one can read a very characteristic statement: "He cannot look at the face, becomes embarrassed when he suddenly feels a gaze directed at him, looks at the ground, or covers his face with his hand."

There are also many healthy young children who do not handle all of this well and show hostility towards adult caresses, often entirely deceptive. They visibly feel uncomfortable when touched, kissed, or held too tightly. They make a very unpleasant grimace, blush, defend themselves if approached energetically, and try to escape. Or if you dominate them, it is clear how tormented and embarrassed they are, and how relieved they are when the procedure is over and they can move away from the aggressive adult. This widespread characteristic in many finely organized children deserves great consideration, and it is precisely against this behavior that excellent educators and pediatricians most often object.

This sensitivity to physical and psychological contact that is too intense can, when abnormally reinforced and distorted in psychopathy, make children particularly difficult to manage and socially unhelpful. Here is an extreme case:

Case 5 Karli St., 7 years old (excerpt from the anamnesis).

He has always been a particularly shy child. If someone looks at him in the street, he already turns his head away. If strangers come into the apartment, he cannot be persuaded to come, he hides or looks out the window. He only looks sideways, in secret. If he receives a gift, he cannot be convinced to say thank you. He has never been to kindergarten, nor with other children, because he only wanted to play with his older sister, who is now 14 years old. He also likes to fight with her. When he is alone, he is capable of having fun, jumping, shouting, and singing. It is only with strangers that he is so difficult.

On the first day of school, he wanted to run away from school. When the teacher tried to bring him back, he struggled with hands and feet. Only on the advice of his mother did he sit on the bench, but he always turned his head away and fiddled with all the buttons on his outfit, embarrassed. Since then, he gets up on time every day and willingly goes to school, but as soon as he sees the teacher, he hides his face. They could not get him to work at school. But at home, he is aware of everything that happens at school and talks about it willingly and proudly. He also dutifully does his homework. According to his mother, he writes, calculates, and draws well.

The child's father, 48 years old, is a drunkard, aggressive, and commits dangerous acts of aggression when angry.

The mother, 49 years old, reports that she too was very shy as a child, hiding under the bed when a stranger came.

Physical: The boy's development is age-appropriate, but he is particularly thin, delicate, and slender, without looking particularly weak. He is particularly gifted in terms of motor skills and shows remarkable agility and skill.

His face is also very finely carved, long and narrow, at first, it was difficult to make him walk, his hair falls in long fringes on his forehead, almost to the eyebrows. When he lowers his head to avoid looking, these fringes form a thick curtain that also protects his eyes.

Internal and neurological organs are normal. No neuropathic stigmata.

The first times after his admission to the service were very difficult. Once the first shock of separation from his mother was over, he retreated to the most protected corner of the playroom, behind the flower table. There he crouched down, invisible from the outside, and only came out for the most important tasks and to sleep. He also slid into this corner to have his meals.

In the nurse's report from the first day, it says: "When taken care of, he was very recalcitrant, during the bath, he struggled with all his might. Then he stayed in a corner for four hours, not looking at anyone and not saying anything. He didn't eat anything today, he cried a lot, it was difficult to put him to bed."

The next day: "Today, he stayed hidden behind the flower table all day. He only ate when his plate was put in his hiding place and there was no one in the room. He didn't cry anymore."

A few days later: "Early on, he had his breakfast nicely. You just have to not look at him, not talk to him. He wouldn't eat either if we didn't give him his plate in his hiding place. He doesn't talk but does everything necessary, like getting dressed, washing, etc. He always puts his hand in front of his face. In the evening, he sits in his bed and only blinks through the gaps between his fingers. Sometimes during the day, he wants to come out of his hiding place behind the flowers; he behaves then like a mouse. He only comes out of his hole when he thinks he is alone. If someone comes, he runs away."

Gradually, over the weeks, I managed to establish contact with him. First, it was the children who triumphantly said that Karli had spoken to them. For a short time, they acted as interpreters between him and the adults and passed on the wishes of each other. Only much later did he start responding to adults and speaking in whispers when he wanted to communicate or show something or needed something. Suddenly, he stood there, head down to hide his face as much as possible, and murmured softly what he had to say before darting away. But until his discharge, addressing an adult he did not know very well remained terribly difficult for him and visibly cost him courage.

Gradually, he began to venture out in public, among the children. He began to participate, at first always ready to escape if a stranger appeared or if someone made a tactical mistake with him. "Later, he participated in all the activities of the children, in gymnastics, games, learning. He no longer enjoyed a position of exception, participated and spoke everywhere, could be lively but also explode and become mean.

When he was ready to speak, he was given an intelligence test. He emerged with a significant intellectual delay, as well as a language disorder. Both aspects had been very well concealed by the psychopathic behavior. He had acclimated well with us and we had learned to accommodate his difficulties and facilitate his social behavior. But of course, he remained psychopathic, and his relationship difficulties were only attenuated, not eliminated. He remained incredibly shy and sensitive until the end. He still tolerated energetic reprimands *better than praise or affection. He turned bright red immediately, hid his head, and sought to escape as quickly as possible. What he disliked most was the full and expressive gaze of an adult. If he was forced to endure it, even in his final and best moments, he made such a grimace that it seemed as if he was suffering from severe physical agony. Until the end, it was impossible to get him to do an activity that put him in the center of general attention and attracted the gaze of many people. The educators were initially as passive as possible towards him, after it was evident from the first days that he did or let happen whatever he considered necessary or relevant to his situation. It quickly became clear that he obeyed orders more easily when given in an impersonal manner and when the content was very concrete. He did not need to be asked, have anything wished of him, be reasoned with, put before a choice, let alone be forced to do something by the power of the gaze. He then hid his face behind his hands or a curtain of hair and refused what was asked of him. And the more he was encouraged, the worse he got. But if the order was given in an indifferent manner, as something obvious, not to be discussed, he did not resist. He also willingly followed when taken by the hand, without being asked for his opinion, and led to the desired place with the words: "I'll give you a hand here: "Now we are going to brush our teeth," "Now Karli will come here and draw." If he had been called gently and enticed: "Karli, come here, don't you want to draw?" or something similar, he would surely have refused.*

If a psychopathic disorder, as in this case, reaches such dimensions that the individual can no longer adapt to society, those around them will have no doubt that it is a pathological behavior. However, if the sensitivity to affective discourse, reprimands, flattery, etc., is not as great, it may manifest in a less visible form, often through a habitual refusal to obey orders, with negativistic traits.

Observing these negativistic children with their parents makes it clear that this insubordinate behavior is provoked by an attitude from the educator that may be correct with other children but is certainly wrong with these particular children. One can regularly witness how the educator, when wanting to demand something from the child, already expects the usual disobedience and therefore attempts from the outset to express their desires in a way that, based on their usual educational experience, is expected to obtain compliance more easily from the reluctant child. They rely on requests, flattery, negotiation, or persuasion. However, these are precisely the forms of influence that this child cannot tolerate. One can deduce from their behavior how difficult and unpleasant the situation is for them. They visibly get irritated, resist in some way, and end up purposefully doing the opposite of what was asked of them, saying no or provocatively doing exactly what was forbidden. Over time, if this repetition persists, negativism becomes a stereotype.

This form of disobedience is also characterized by the fact that the child is willing to correct the educator's behavior. If addressed in an objective and impersonal manner, surprising achievements can be obtained from them, and over time, the negativism tends to fade. Such an impersonal attitude towards the child does not mean monotonous, boring, or hostile behavior. One can have fun with the child, offer various things, be firm with them, joke with them, in short, be open and in good contact with them while avoiding offering or demanding displays of friendship, affection, and tenderness.

The pronounced forms of this negativism are never exclusively exogenous. They are almost always the expression of a severe psychopathic condition. Consequently, any mistakes made by the educators are only relative. One should not expect a surprising cure by acting correctly, but rather a considerable improvement in the child's social adaptation. If this improvement is sustainable, it represents crucial assistance for the child and their educators.

LANGUAGE AND AFFECTIVE CONTACT (1943)

This article is an attempt to analyze several familiar types of language disorders in children. It is assumed that isolated disorders of different language components will highlight their respective values by demonstrating what does not work, or does not work properly, in each particular case. Such analysis should also show specific difficulties that result from these isolated disorders. Language forms the basis of all social relationships, and alterations in social relationships between the child and adults, the child and other children, and the child and social groups can be expected as a consequence of these dysfunctions.

The contrast between what a child says and how they say it

Let's suppose that a number of children narrate the same unpleasant events at home. We assume that they all faithfully describe what happened and use the same words. Even in this case, each child will present their story differently and allow us to recognize what they truly feel. One child will try not to be overwhelmed by emotions while narrating. These unsuccessful efforts to control themselves reveal the strength of their feelings. Another child will tremble with anger at the mere mention of what was done to them, expressing their deep sense of being wronged. A third child will recite their story with exaggerated tragic gestures, showing that speaking and complaining about past sufferings ultimately provide a certain pleasure. The narration of events at

68

home can be recited in a monotonous manner, as something that was painful long ago but has become a desperately indifferent daily event. The child may tell their story in a chatty manner, obviously not expressing their own opinions and feelings but merely repeating what they heard at home or from neighbors. Some children report their story with remarkably impersonal objectivity, as if narrating not their own experiences but someone else's story. The report may even be made cheerfully and amid much laughter, proving that the terrible events recounted have not deeply impressed this child.

In all these cases, the examiner gains two different sets of information. By listening to the child's words, they learn what happened - the objective facts. At the same time, they recognize what the child truly feels about these events, even if their feelings are not verbalized. Other means of communication beyond words are used for this purpose. The same coexistence of factual and emotional content can be demonstrated in the language of an adult giving an order to a child. The content and meaning of an order, even if its verbal and grammatical structure is definitively established, are by no means invariant. Its meaning can undergo radical changes depending on how it is expressed. The same phrase, "Please come here," can be an occasional request, a call for help, an emphatic repetition of a given order, a cry of excitement or anger, a threatening announcement of punishment, or a sigh of despair after many previous failures.

The particular meaning of this order, and of any other, depends on how it is expressed. One cannot know, or only vaguely know, the intentions of a giver of the order as long as the order is considered solely in its written form and detached from the actual situation in which it is given. There is no doubt about its underlying meaning and intention when a precise form of expression is added to its words, just as one cannot assess the full weight of a child's report on their sufferings at home without judging both the factual and emotional content of what they say.

It is well known that human language possesses, in addition to words, numerous other symbols that are as universally accepted, used, and understood as words. The question arises of what happens if an individual is unable to use these nonverbal symbols.

Parkinsonian Language Disorder

A particular form of language results from Parkinsonian motor disorder, as encountered in children suffering from post-encephalitic affection. Its well-known symptoms are as follows: (1) Parkinsonian language is not accompanied by (a) mimetic gestures, or (b) gestural movements of the arms and trunk; (2) it is not modulated, meaning the usual changes in force and pitch of the voice are absent.

The face and body of the Parkinsonian patient remain immobile while speaking, and their speech flows with a constant, gentle monotony. Their words come out as if from a mask that has replaced their once lively and expressive face, or like from a lifeless statue inside of which hides a speech automaton. Their lips barely move while speaking. Only the eyes retain their original vivid motility, looking around, shining when amused or mischievous, bright when appreciating something.

From the absence of gestures and modulation in the voice results an automaton-like language, devoid of the usual expressiveness and meaning. Upon hearing and seeing it, one feels perplexed, not knowing what is missing.

What is missing in this language? The Parkinsonian patient sees something funny and is amused, but neither gestures nor sounds of laughter appear. They are discontent or unhappy, but what they say does not seem depressed, and their face does not show sadness. They cry, but one can only recognize it if tears flow on their immobile face. A person being addressed by them feels insecure, not knowing if the patient is friendly, hostile, or indifferent, as no gestures of friendliness or aversion appear on their face, nor any expression of these feelings in their voice.

If a Parkinsonian child were to narrate their unpleasant experiences at home, one would understand what happened - the objective facts. However, one would not be able to recognize what they truly feel about these events because, like any other child, they cannot express these feelings through gestures or modulation of their voice.

If a Parkinsonian adult patient were to give an order to a child, the child would be unable to know how the order was meant, as, in the absence of gestures and expressive inflections, the important implications of urgency, severity, kindness, threat, or jest would not be perceivable.

Parkinsonian patients can perform all gestural movements they explicitly focus their attention on. They can execute the grimaces of crying, laughing, anger, threat, just as they are capable of executing any other of their formerly automated motor patterns if an order directs their attention to it. However, they cannot perform gestures involuntarily, authentically linked to the corresponding feeling or emotion.

The Two Systems of Language Symbols

We are accustomed to reading on a partner's face and recognizing in the slightest nuances the ever-changing feelings, moods, affects, and emotions they experience during a conversation or shared activity. Only exceptionally do they communicate these in words. Usually, they do not report "I am joyful," "I feel good," "I like you." They are even rarely conscious of these feelings. If they are, the affect, emotion, mood, or sentiment has already been objectified. Through an introspective act that is no longer the emotion itself, the feeling has been elevated to clear consciousness and transformed into a thought reflecting on that emotion. However, we generally express our emotions through symbols other than words, without explicit intention. The person we converse with can see that we are in a good mood, that we feel good, or that we like them. The nonverbal symbols through which we express these emotions are as universally accepted and understood as spoken words. The means of this expression are the accentuation and modulation of spoken words, as well as accompanying gestures.

The following rule is generally valid: thoughts that are elevated to clear consciousness are communicated through spoken words. Feelings, moods, affects, and emotions are expressed, more or less involuntarily, through other specific symbols - mimetic gestures, body gestures, and modulation of speech. The spoken or written word will be referred to as verbal language, and the triad of mimetic gestures, body gestures, and speech modulation will be called emotional language.

In addition to this triad of emotional language, there is another essential indicator of the individual's emotional state: the accompanying vegetative reactions - blushing, paleness, pupil constriction and dilation, changes in breathing rhythm, tears secretion, etc. These reactions do not disappear in the case of Parkinsonism. After the degradation of the patient's emotional language, they can serve as the last indicator of their true emotional state. However, these vegetative reactions do not seem to have the strict and exclusive purpose of being means of communication like the symbols of emotional language. Verbal language and emotional language disappear when an individual is alone or, for some reason, isolated from the people around them. Vegetative reactions appear in relation to the corresponding emotions even in solitary individuals and patients whose contact with others is continuously interrupted, and therefore, they never use communicative symbols.

Verbal language and emotional language are integrated into the indivisible whole of human language. However, there are several conditions in which one of these two systems of symbols is isolated, separated from its non-functional partner. Parkinson's syndrome is the classic example of a condition in which verbal language continues to function after emotional language has been abolished.

On the other hand, there are several pathological and non-pathological conditions in which emotional language is preserved or even intensified compensating for the absence of words.

Emotional Language in Isolation

1. Deaf-Mutism.

The only means of communication remaining for deaf-mute children are facial expressions and body gestures, which play an exceptional role as communication supports between them and other people. Intelligent deaf-mute children use more pronounced and emphasized gestures than individuals with intact hearing. They also intentionally use many gestural symbols, similar to how others use words. These new symbols do not express emotions but represent concrete objects, qualities, or activities—concepts that, under normal conditions, are represented by verbal symbols. Wherever deaf-mutes form a community, they develop a set of gestural symbols, an extensive vocabulary encompassing special signs for all concrete concepts of a primitive language. These signs are well understood and correctly used by members of this community (for example, in a school for deaf-mute children), while a stranger would be unable to grasp the meaning of most of them. The correct use and understanding of voice modulation depend on the ability to hear, just as the correct understanding and use of words do. Deaf individuals can, with the help of their other senses, learn to understand and say words, but they never learn to use proper voice inflection. Their voice remains hoarse and monotonous, and they speak at an unusual pitch throughout their lives.

2. Congenital Word Deafness

This is another pathological condition in which emotional language is isolated. Children who suffer from this condition are unable to understand and pronounce words, even if they have good hearing; most often, they are partially deaf. However, they can understand the meaning of other organized sounds (music, everyday noises). These children cannot speak and do not comprehend the meaning of words, but they use and understand emotional language symbols, including the modulation of spoken words. It is surprising to see how much they can read from the speaker's face and how adept they are at acting and behaving accordingly. They are perfectly capable of expressing their primitive ideas through lively gestures and an expressive yet inarticulate "baby talk." Without using words, they manage to establish good relationships with the people around them and adapt quite well to daily routines. Parents often report that the child, though unable to speak, "understands every word said to them." In reality, they do not understand a single word, or at best, only a few. As soon as the speaker artificially eliminates emotional language by speaking in a monotone, expressionless manner, the child suddenly becomes unable to grasp what is being said. They also fail if prevented from looking at the speaker. Unlike deaf-mute children, those with congenital word deafness not only use mimetic and body gestures as a means of communication but also intonations of their voice. When they try to say something, it sounds as if they are speaking with emphasis in a foreign language. It quickly becomes evident that they are using meaningless idioglossia. They produce sounds that resemble words and assemble them into sequences of sounds that resemble phrases. These sound formations devoid of meaning serve as support for a well-developed emotional language. Through the expressive intonation of these sounds and the proper raising and lowering of the voice, these children perfectly convey their real emotional state and are quite capable of communicating their desires and intentions and can even provide some primitive factual information.

3. Infants' Language

There is a transitional stage in the development of any healthy child, during which all these symptoms of the aphasic group are present. An emotional connection between the mother and the baby is established several months before the baby starts speaking, from the first appearance of a smile of recognition. This connection is established through the numerous sounds and gestural symbols characteristic of the baby's exclusively emotional language. It develops and differentiates further during the first year of life and reaches its peak at the time of "baby talk." Infants' babbling is one of the examples of perfect speech modulation existing separately from its usual substrate, words.

4. Dogs' Language

The relationship between a dog and its owner is governed by an elaborate system of gestural symbols and expressive sounds, though not necessarily articulated ones. A dog can express all kinds of feelings, affects, and emotions through highly differentiated body gestures and barking sounds. It is also capable of recognizing its owner's moods, intentions, friendly and unfriendly feelings and acting accordingly. However, even the most intelligent dog understands very few words. It is a well-known trick to address a dog with words of the most unfriendly content but say them with a gentle voice and caressing gestures. The dog will accept them as kindness, even be delighted, jump, and wag its tail, proving that it acts solely based on gestures and the modulation of words, but does not register their verbal meaning.

Consequences of Verbal and Emotional Language Disorders

Verbal language and emotional language are means of communication that only become meaningful in the presence of another person capable of receiving and interpreting their generally accepted and understood symbols. Any disturbance in either language can, therefore, lead to a form of disorder in the patient's relationships with other people. The symptoms of the disorder differ fundamentally with respect to each of the two languages.

1. Verbal Language

(a) Expressing thoughts through words for the purpose of communication is an act that the speaker is fully aware of.

(b) A patient who loses this ability immediately realizes their loss.

(c) A mute person is immediately recognized as such by anyone who has tried to speak with them.

In other words, both the patient and the people in their environment are fully aware of the abnormal situation and its implications. Efforts to overcome and compensate for the difficulty are made more or less consciously, and there is no room for misinterpretation or misunderstanding.

2. Emotional Language

(a) A person who expresses their real feelings through emotional language symbols is not aware or barely aware that they are doing so; they also do not know much about their ability to use these symbols as a means of communication.

(b) They do not recognize the loss of their emotional language, which has been abolished. The Parkinson's patient is capable of feeling joy or sadness, but like any other person, they do not care whether their happiness or sorrow is visible on their face. They probably do not even know that something is wrong with their language.

(c) A person speaking with such a patient will notice that something in their partner's behavior is unusual, but they will not recognize the emotional language disorder as such. Very characteristic misunderstandings are a consequence of this.

One cannot help drawing conclusions about a person's emotional state from their emotional language. You look at their face, hear their voice, and instantly know what mood they are in or what they feel. You only make mistakes if a person's attitude, gestures, and voice modulation do not express their emotions (a "poker face" is an example). In such a case, either one suspects concealment, or one automatically assumes that the emotional reaction did not occur at all, and negative qualities corresponding to the immobility of their face and the monotony of their language are attributed to the patient. A Parkinson's patient is considered insensitive if they experience pain without a defensive reaction and without any distortion of their face. They appear indifferent or apathetic if they witness an exciting event with an expressionless face and a motionless body. They seem impudent or challenging if, instead of obeying an order, they stare at the teacher without any sign of obedience. Similar misunderstandings constantly occur between Parkinson's children and their teachers.

Differential Symptomatology of the Two Groups of Speech Disorders

I would like to differentiate the symptoms of these two groups of speech disorders, one in which verbal language is damaged while emotional language is preserved (deaf-mutism, congenital word deafness, etc.), and the other in which only emotional language is destroyed (post-encephalitic parkinsonism).

Group 1 : Aphasia Group

1. Children in this group are, of course, unable to speak verbal language.

2. They have no understanding of words or limited comprehension.

3. They are capable of speaking emotional language and using it as a means of communication.

4. They can understand emotional language spoken by others.

5. Despite linguistic difficulties, it is possible to establish good personal relationships with them. Whenever one addresses them or they address us, it feels like being in good contact with them.

6. Communicating factual knowledge is difficult since words, the natural instruments of symbolizing facts, are absent. This is true even for highly intelligent deaf-mute or aphasic individuals. They can formulate and communicate factual knowledge only through gesticulations and interjections that are inferior substitutes for lacking word symbols.

Group 2 : Parkinsonism Group

1. Parkinson's patients are capable of speaking verbal language.

2. They understand it.

What about emotional language and personal contact? It is possible to establish fairly good personal relationships with a

Parkinson's patient. The experience of not being in good contact with them only occurs when one meets them for the first time, feeling bewildered by the strange immobility of their body, their masked face, and the monotony and lack of expression in their language. One understands their words but does not really know what they mean, what they feel, or what their intentions are.

These difficulties disappear as one gets to know them better. One learns to recognize what they feel, even if they do not express it through gestures. Various small signs replace the absent gestural symbols: vegetative and vasomotor reactions, the manner and nature of their actions, verbalizations of emotions. A reasonably good contact eventually develops, despite the absence of emotional language. The patient makes this possible through their attitude. Like a healthy child, they strive to establish relationships with people; they want to communicate and receive communications, play with other children, participate in their activities, amusements, and experiences. They follow with interest what people around them do, are capable of understanding what they think and feel, and react with appropriate thoughts and feelings. Thus, they become an integral part of the social group they belong to and can resonate with their emotions.

It is only partially correct to say that these children lack emotional language. They cannot speak it, but they receive and understand its symbols, to which they respond with appropriate emotions. Only the executional organ that should manifest these emotions and communicate them to others is destroyed. Therefore

3. Parkinson's patients are unable to speak emotional language symbols.

4. However, they are capable of understanding them.

5. Their personal contact with people exists, although it is different from normal contact and is established with some difficulty. It can even be quite good, provided that the two partners in contact know each other well enough.

6. The communication of factual knowledge is disrupted.

7. The tendency for communication is normal.

<u>Lack of Contact with People</u>

Similar viewpoints to those applied in the analysis of the group of aphasics and the group of Parkinson's patients will now be used for the discussion of a third group, of which the following case is a raw example.

The boy, Karl K., was seen at regular intervals between his sixth and thirteenth year. The clinical diagnosis of tuberous sclerosis was established from the beginning. The skin around his nose showed the characteristic eruptions of sebaceous adenomas. He suffered from petit mal seizures from a very young age and from grand mal seizures starting at the age of ten. He was mentally impaired.

He was a robust, well-built boy with primitive facial features and a dull expression. His physical development had been good during all those years of observation, not different from that of a healthy boy.

He did not speak at all. Never in his life did he utter a word or make a sound. It was known only through his appropriate responses to certain primitive verbal commands that he understood some words and phrases. He would come when offered something pleasant; he would run away when asked to do something he disliked. No other access to him existed beyond these limited possibilities, as he neither responded nor reacted to any form of address, be it words, gestures, or calls. His expression remained blank, he did not look at the face of the person calling him, he did not turn towards or away from them. A strong defensive reaction only appeared if the person was very aggressive, doing something he disliked, or if they annoyed him by speaking. In such cases, he would try to break free, push the aggressor away, or run away. One could deduce from the swiftness of his movements, rather than from symbolic communication, that the intrusion bothered him. He was never seen to spontaneously address a person. Never in his life did he smile, laugh, or cry; he never became aggressive in anger or expressed any other emotion. He showed no interest in people, nor a glance that would express curiosity, doubt, a wish, affection, or aversion.

After a superficial examination, one might have suspected that he was deaf. However, it was known that he could hear because he responded appropriately to various non-verbal acoustic stimuli and later in childhood developed a primitive understanding of words.

Karl was first seen in a hospital ward among sick and mostly bedridden children. He had to be kept in a closed bed in which he seemed to feel very well. His days passed in a monotonous void, paradoxically combined with constant pseudo-activity. He jumped around, swayed in a sitting or standing position, or made other rhythmic movements.

As soon as an attempt was made to take him out of his bed, he showed the typical behavior of a hyperactive and mentally impaired child. He would run like lightning as soon as his bed was opened and from then on, he kept moving continuously around the large room. He approached the bed of a young girl and, *without changing his expression or saying a word, grabbed her hair, let go again, and left before the bewildered girl even realized what had happened. He approached another bed, took a toy from a child's hand, turned it and stared at it for a few seconds, then dropped it, moved to a table where some medications and instruments were prepared for use, and threw them into disarray. He continued like this incessantly and at dizzying speed.*

He somewhat calmed down during his stay in the ward. Not through symbolic communication but through his appropriate actions in respective situations, for example, his appropriate use of a spoon, cooperative movements of his body and arms while dressing, an appropriate fighting reaction when faced with an unwanted event, one could conclude that he had learned to understand the purposes of many everyday events and objects. Observing his actions was crucial, as he never expressed his thoughts through words or other communicative symbols. This was the reason why everyone considered him even more mentally impaired than he actually was.

I used to visit and examine him in his home. There, he was less agitated and his behavior was more determined than in the hospital. He was well aware of the day's events and had a well-established daily routine. There were things he wanted to do and did regularly. He had somewhere, at the top of a shelf, a place where he liked to sit; he knew where it was allowed and forbidden to climb, where he could find food. His mother even allowed him to leave the house unaccompanied, as he always stayed within the house, never caused any damage, and never ran into danger.

He was less agitated and better adjusted in this familiar environment. The most striking was the contrast between this relatively reasonable behavior and the total absence of relationships with the people around him, even with his mother. The changing immobility and indifference of his face, the constant emptiness of his gaze, the absence of words and sounds were astonishing and made everyone uncomfortable when attempting to communicate with him. They were confronted with a being that looked like a human creature, often behaved like one, but lacked a specifically human quality: the ability to communicate with others and engage in social relations with them.

Diagnostic evaluation of Karl K. would probably be: tuberous sclerosis with its characteristic symptoms of sebaceous adenoma, symptomatic epilepsy, idiocy, and organic drive. The case, seen from this perspective, is simple and not very interesting. The reason we describe it in this context is that the phenomenon of a lack of contact with people is represented with rare clarity. The boy's attitude towards the people around him is very unusual. This particular behavior would not be properly characterized as "idiocy," "mutism," or "aphasia."

This language disorder is entirely different from that of the other two groups. The boy resembled an aphasic individual in not using words and having an extremely limited understanding of words. However, addressing him with symbols of emotional language was equally ineffective, and like Parkinsonian patients, he did not use facial gestures or other gestures.

He neither received nor emitted any symbols of communication. This is an impressive phenomenon: a boy who undoubtedly sees and hears, yet pays no attention to a person who clearly and conspicuously enters the field of his senses and addresses him. Conversely, establishing some form of relationship, whether through a barely perceptible smile, a nod, a brief exchange of glances, a friendly or impatient attitude, is so understood and integrated into human relationships that we don't even realize its presence when it is there. We are perplexed and sense that something is amiss only when the expected reaction does not occur.

Difference in attitude towards people and towards objects. The boy's behavior among playing children is a good example of what is meant by this. His mother used to bring him to the outpatient clinic. There, he had to wait in a large room where many other children were playing alone or in groups. This noisy and strange environment increased his agitation. He kept moving constantly, touching and manipulating all the objects that came into his perception. The children were among these objects: he touched them, looked at them, took their toys. He did this just as he would touch and fixate on the blocks scattered on the floor. He took a doll from a girl's hand just as he would have taken it from a table. In doing so, he didn't look at her face, didn't smile, didn't threaten, didn't attack her, and didn't defend himself.

He roamed among all these children like a strange being, crossing their groups and circles without interest, without trying to learn anything about them or tell them something. He didn't participate in their games, he didn't even seem to notice them. Sometimes, he would destroy one of their toys. It was never clear whether it was a mere incident or a deliberate act of destruction.

His attitude towards children and also towards the adults around him was similar to that which healthy

individuals adopt towards objects in their environment. With objects, one does what is necessary, uses them if they are useful, eliminates them if they are harmful. But one does not communicate with them, nor expect communication from them. Words and symbols of emotional language are only directed at beings considered capable of thinking and experiencing just like oneself. A solitary person, i.e., someone surrounded only by objects, does not express thoughts and feelings; they are silent, do not make gestures, and their attitude is closed. The motor organs for executing their verbal and emotional language are temporarily not used, for the same reason that they were not used permanently in Karl's case. They start functioning the moment the person comes into contact with someone. To convince yourself of this, just observe a person who, while working alone at their desk or walking alone on the street, is accosted by someone. At that moment, their closed face lights up, and they begin to express what is in their mind.

It is generally considered that a person who talks to themselves is somewhat peculiar. The monologue in a classic play is a good example. Its lack of naturalness is mainly due to the fact that a person speaks aloud, with a lot of pathos and strong gestures, when alone. In reality, no one would confide their thoughts, no matter how beautiful, or their feelings, no matter how intense, to a deserted solitude.

The boy affected by tuberous sclerosis, even in the midst of a crowd of people, behaved like a loner. For him, human beings did not seem distinct from lifeless objects in their particular quality of animation and personalization. Therefore, he did not communicate with them. He did not address them because he could not perceive them as individuals. Unlike a Parkinson's patient, he was not deprived of his emotional language due to the corresponding motor function being destroyed. Instead, he did not use this function, even though it was practically intact.

Any healthy individual feels, at least at certain times, the desire to break free from the solitude surrounding them in an inanimate environment. There is an inherent communicative tendency, the inclination to establish and maintain relationships with people and human communities. This tendency, present in all mentally sound individuals, is preserved in deaf-mutes, aphasics, Parkinson's patients, and the majority of intellectually impaired children. It is due to this inclination that they all try to compensate for the partial loss of their symbolic functions by intensifying and amplifying the remaining ones.

However, the boy affected by tuberous sclerosis never showed reactions that could be interpreted as attempts to establish relationships with others. The tendency to communicate was completely absent.

In summary, the symptoms of the speech disorder in this case, representing the extreme form of the lack of contact with others, are as follows:

1. The boy did not speak verbal language at all.

2. He had an extremely limited understanding of words.

3. He did not express any symbols of emotional language.

4. He was insensitive to the symbols of emotional language

directed at him.

5. One experienced a lack of emotional contact with him in his presence.

6. His factual relations with others were very restricted.

7. He behaved as if he was unable to experience people as different from inanimate objects.

8. He had no inclination to communicate.

As a result, almost all connections between him and his human environment were severed, while relatively numerous relationships existed between him and the objects surrounding him.

This situation is reversed in the majority of intellectually impaired children. Their disorder, the lack of intelligence, is primarily an inability to understand the meaning of events, facts, objects, and their causal and logical relationships. The emotional and affective life of these children and their emotional relationships with people may be normal; in any case, they are less disturbed than their factual relationships with objects, people, and situations.

This predominance of the disturbance in emotional contact over intellectual impairment is characteristic of all cases of this type, and the disorder in contact should not be interpreted as a mere consequence of the lack of intelligence. The case described is a rather extreme example in this regard. The boy's intelligence was also at an extremely low level. He fell at the lower end of a series of cases that share the disturbance in emotional contact, but whose intelligence varies from idiocy to the remarkable and specific performances of a certain type of prodigious child.

People with impaired intelligence but highly differentiated affective life and excellent contact with others have often been described in literary works. The combination of touching helplessness and intuitive understanding of others' suffering, their ethical superiority, and their eventual victory over intelligent but cold and ruthless adversaries make them valuable motifs. Examples of this type can be found in almost all of Dickens' novels: Mr. Dick in David Copperfield, Maggie in Little Dorrit, and Barnaby Rudge. Perhaps the most famous example is Dostoevsky's The Idiot.

CONCLUSION

We attempted to reanalyze several familiar types of childhood language disorders: purely motor disorders of post-encephalitic parkinsonism; acoustic disorders of deaf-mutism and congenital verbal deafness; and several other pathological and physiological conditions in which language is not yet or not at all developed. Finally, the case of a severely impaired child suffering from an essential inability to form social and emotional relationships was examined in more detail. Particular interest was given to the question of how the language of gestures was affected in each case. It turned out that gestural language, although less visible, has no less important function than that of words: to symbolize objective facts and communicate them to others. Gestures, not words, are the appropriate symbols of emotions, affects, and moods. Precise and well-described disturbances in the individual's relationships with others result from gestural language disorders. Only extreme cases that are easily amenable to analysis were addressed in this article. However, the author believes that a similar analysis will be heuristic in many other less abnormal cases showing similar disturbances in affective and social relationships.

We have become accustomed to considering gestures as a somewhat superfluous relic from a time when the ancestors of Homo sapiens, lacking words and in need of some means of communication, used motor and vegetative-motor reactions to intimidate their enemies and attract their friends. This description only reveals the origin or gestural symbols as a means of communication. But our cases show that gestures are not simply a transient remnant of ancient times. It seems, instead, that the communication of emotions through gestural symbols is an important and well-established function that is by no means destined to disappear as long as emotions play a significant role in human interrelationships.

AUTISM IN CHILDHOOD: AN ATTEMPT OF AN ANALYSIS (1957)

INTRODUCTION

It is now certain that the overall impression we have come to recognize as early childhood psychosis, or childhood schizophrenia, or early infantile autism, is not truly a nosological unit. Our efforts to define it as a physical disease following Virchow's principles or as a mental disease following Kraepelin's principles have misled us. They have led us exactly to the same difficulties and contradictions that our efforts to define adult schizophrenia as a pathological entity suffered from for many years.

It is possible, of course, that one day a significant medical discovery will be made, clearly defining a disease like "infantile schizophrenia." Someone may discover a deficiency of a newly identified hormone that always accompanies the clinical picture of early infantile schizophrenia; the destruction of a region, a layer, or a type of cells in the central nervous system, yet to be identified, might be closely correlated with autistic changes in preschool age; a specific constitutional anomaly might be regarded as the decisive predisposing factor for the development of the syndrome; or another yet unpredictable pathology of the body might be detected as a regular correlate to the psychopathological picture of infantile schizophrenia as we see it today.

Such a discovery would justify the assumption of a causal link between the physical disorder and the psychopathological syndrome. The disease, clearly definable, with both physical and psychopathological characteristics, could then be called "infantile schizophrenia." However, we are certainly not there yet.

Nevertheless, even such a discovery would not change the fact that identical or very similar personality changes - schizophrenic or autistic symptoms of early childhood - can also occur as a result of other pathological conditions in the body, and most likely as a consequence of severe environmental damage in early childhood. In fact, a combination of several of these causative factors may be found in many cases, if not all cases, of infantile schizophrenia. The roundtable on infantile schizophrenia during the orthopsychiatric meeting in Cleveland in 1953, which involved numerous distinguished authors in the field, highlighted our current uncertainty about the origin and causes of this condition. For now, we still have to regard infantile psychosis as a purely psychological concept, not a nosological one. It is a pathological state of mind. Even as such, we have been able to apprehend it only intuitively, as a total impression.

Our current enthusiastic concern for genetic-dynamic principles has made us forget that our theories about the origin and causes of adult schizophrenia rest on the solid and reliable foundations of what is now called "Kraepelinian psychiatry," sometimes with a slightly disparaging nuance. Our theories would be mere speculations without the careful descriptions and phenomenological analyses done by the psychiatrists of that past period. Such a reliable base of descriptions does not yet exist for the psychotic states of early childhood. Few attempts have been made to develop detailed and comprehensive descriptions of Kanner's early infantile autism. The same applies to Mahler's "symbiotic psychosis." In contrast, discussions about various hypotheses regarding the origin and causes of infantile schizophrenia are plentiful. At times, it seems that the respective hypotheses and assumptions have slipped in merely as a reflection of the author's school of thought. The implicit demand that they be taken for granted is present. A child analyst has a completely different view of the problem of infantile psychosis than the director of a major child psychiatric center in a metropolitan area. In a way, that's how it should be. The differences in viewpoints have allowed attention to focus on different aspects of the disorder. However, premature - I am tempted to say detrimental - focus on one facet of a complex issue also has its dangers. The author's preoccupying theory can act like blinkers, causing phenomena that do not fit the theory to disappear.

A temporary return to the stage of description and then phenomenological analysis seems desirable regarding infantile psychoses. This should not be interpreted as a rejection of the genetic-dynamic perspective. It indicates a desire to regain control.

Such a return is intended in this article. It is first intended to describe, and perhaps phenomenologically analyze, a restricted but certainly central part of the infantile schizophrenia syndrome: autism. Such an attempt does not seem to have been made in recent years, since Minkowsky's in-depth and revealing investigations.

Minkowsky's efforts resulted in resignation. He came to the conclusion that the phenomena he called "emotional contact with the environment" and "emotional contact with people" could no longer be reduced to their elements by analysis. Approaching a person in conversation, or in shared activity with them, one experiences successively the phenomena of "good contact," "difficult contact," or "no relationship can be established." The entirety of this stimulating impression can be described.

Minkowsky, Kretschmer, Kraepelin, Bleuler, and others did this masterfully. Afterward, however, it must be accepted as such. It particularly resists attempts at psychological analysis. The same is true for Jung's popular pairs of terms "extraversion - introversion" and Kretschmer's "cyclothymic - schizothymic." The character types these expressions refer to are experienced as such when encountering a person who embodies the prototype. A positive correlation between character types and bodily types could be established. Beyond that, the experience of a disturbance in emotional contact between two people proves resistant to other attempts at analysis.

The psychopathological term "autism," though closely linked to the concepts of "breakdown of emotional contact," "introversion," and "schizoid," refers to a different aspect of the problem. Bleuler saw something else in autism than a simply describable but indefinable and analyzable aspect of the schizophrenic person. He saw it as a specific state of mind in which the person is different and thinks differently from a non-autistic person. A subtle shift in the meaning of the term has occurred since Bleuler coined it. The expressions "autism" and "autistic" are used in recent psychiatric literature as quite general, loosely defined, descriptive terms, approximately synonymous with the expressions "withdrawal" and "self-absorption," which are so frequently used to describe what happens to a person when they become schizophrenic.

These terms suffer from a lack of clear definition. Their meaning seems to be at times: "withdrawal from contact with reality"; more frequently: "withdrawal from contact with people." They often appear - rather improperly - to denote not something that happens to the person but something they actively do. It appears as though they intentionally withdraw from something that has become unbearable; as if they deliberately close themselves off from something they can no longer cope with.

We will attempt to discuss and support the following thesis in this article:

(1) Autism can be defined and understood, in line with Bleuler, as a specific state of mind;

(2) This state of mind is not necessarily abnormal;

(3) The state of autism has its complement in the state of "communication with people." One is either in one state or the other;

(4) The mentally healthy person can freely move, unknowingly, from the state of communication with others to the state of autism, whereas a person with pathological autism is - more or less - trapped in this condition. The transition from the state of autism to a living and communicative relationship with people causes them great difficulties or discomfort, as long as the establishment of such a relationship is still possible.

CHAPTER I

Some characteristics of the language of autistic children will be described in this first part of the study, and an attempt will be made to analyze them and formulate some of the specific psychopathological mechanisms that cause these symptoms. Severe cases of autism will serve as the starting point for these discussions. A fully developed pathology offers the advantage of highlighting the essential qualities of the concerned syndrome.

The reader may notice, perhaps with some annoyance, that we have adhered to a descriptive, almost behavioral level in this part of our discussion. This has been done partly by choice. The desire to create a relatively unbiased factual basis played a role in this self-restriction. However, it is also important to keep in mind that empathic understanding of extremely autistic individuals is very difficult, if not impossible.

A very different approach is planned for the second part of the study. Only cases with minor, temporary, or permanent loosening of their connection with people will be examined, with an emphasis on the phenomenological perspective.

PART I: CHARACTERISTICS OF AUTISTIC MUTISM

The following is a description of certain aspects of the behavior of a child whose contact with the people around him has been almost completely interrupted as much as possible. These not-so-rare cases of extreme autism in early childhood bear a striking resemblance in appearance and symptomatology. They all present the same monotonous clinical picture, unlike the colorful and varied symptomatology of pathological cases of early infantile autism, which are less extensive, and also cases where compensatory and restorative processes have taken place. The essential characteristics of autistic language can be particularly clearly highlighted here, given that the syndrome has been so fully developed.

Case 1

The boy we are thinking of here, Johnny, is now seven years old. He would have developed normally - even precociously - during his early childhood and until about two and a half years old. Sitting, walking, and toilet training would have developed normally. His mother insists that he started saying words at the end of his first year, and his language continued to develop steadily afterward. He could form short sentences and put phrases together at the age of two. Then, he gradually stopped talking. He has remained mute since then.

The mother describes how Johnny also withdrew during this period and how he would sit motionless for hours. There has been little change since. The boy comes from a poor family. There are mental illnesses among his close and distant relatives. The family unit, consisting of the father, mother, and five children with Johnny being the fourth, is poorly integrated. They live on a meager income. The social agency that has been working with the family for many years describes the mother as a difficult, neurotic person who is not interested in her family and neglects household chores. Her attitude towards Johnny is described as an erratic mix of overprotection and hostile mismanagement.

This historical summary is, of course, very inadequate. It would leave many questions open if we were concerned here with the etiology of the disease. However, as mentioned above, this case serves solely as material for a description and an attempt to analyze the phenomenon of "extreme autism." It is also intended to give the reader an idea of the type of cases we have in mind in this chapter.

The following questions will be discussed using this case and others in this chapter: How does the extremely autistic child communicate, or not communicate, with the people around him? And assuming there is a disorder or defect in the realm of communication, how can it be described and formulated in scientific terms? What are the specific qualities of language or mutism in these children?

I was introduced to Johnny and his mother in the waiting room of an outpatient clinic. There was no one else there at that time. Johnny stood near his mother but at a certain distance from her. He turned and looked at me when I arrived, perhaps to gauge my intentions. Then he turned away. I couldn't tell if he did it out of indifference or deliberately to avoid being addressed. I informed his mother that our interview would take place in a room upstairs. She turned to Johnny and said, "Come on, Johnny, let's go upstairs." In the following seconds, I had the impression that Johnny had not taken note of that order. He did not react at all initially. His mother didn't seem particularly bothered by it. She appeared used to it. She did not repeat the order but got up, paying no attention to Johnny, and we began to head towards the stairs. However, Johnny also started moving. He ran up the stairs ahead of us. There, he found himself in unfamiliar territory. He waited for us, then followed at a certain distance and eventually watched us settle into the chairs. He did not say a word, and there was not a single expression on his face while he did all this. So, it was impossible for me to know what he was feeling. Only his actions confirmed beyond a doubt that he had understood his mother's order. The mother paid no further attention to him upstairs. When I asked somewhat concerned, she casually replied that he would be fine. She was right. He wandered aimlessly in the hallway and the adjacent empty examination rooms for a while. Then he settled into a chair in the nearby room, not far from where we were sitting.

I want to focus the discussion on this simple event: The mother said to Johnny, "Come on, Johnny, let's go upstairs." I had the impression that Johnny did not heed that order. A few seconds later, I was surprised to see him heading towards the stairs in front of us. He had heard and understood his mother after all. I felt astonished.

Why had I initially thought Johnny had not heard or at least paid attention to that order, and why was I surprised later when I realized he had understood? Something crucial must have been missing in his reaction.

We take it for granted that something will happen before and during a person's reaction to an order by taking appropriate action. We first expect them to communicate to us how they received the order and what they intend to do with it. This communicative reaction to the mother's order did not happen in Johnny's case. This automatically made me assume he hadn't heard. I had to correct that impression when he reacted with a non-communicative, appropriate action a few moments later.

This behavior and the interpretational misunderstanding it causes are characteristic of extremely autistic children. It can be formulated in the following general terms: In any situation where people are gathered in a shared activity (this term being used here in its widest possible sense), there is a continuous exchange of communications flowing between them, conveying factual information, announcing intentions of action, expressing feelings towards the current situation, and - most importantly - communicatively expressing feelings towards the person with whom one is engaged in the shared activity. It is this continuous, visible, and audible flow and exchange of communications that distinguishes, for an observer, a person in social contact from a solitary or autistic person. Whenever we find ourselves in a situation requiring social contact with another person, we take it for granted that such a flow of communicative exchanges will occur. We misinterpret or feel perplexed, uncertain, and powerless when it does not come. Something essential is missing. In Johnny's case, this was true.

The reader may object: It is common for people to obey or disobey orders without saying a word. One can join in a shared activity, for example, work for hours in unison and good contact, without ever saying a word. This is absolutely true. But these people are still communicating. Let's consider the following example: A child is told to do something. He then looks straight into the face of the adult giving the order. He does it with a stubborn expression, tightens his lips, and his body stiffens as if to say, "I won't move!" This child does not say a word. In fact, he actively refuses to speak. Yet, we cannot accuse him of not communicating. He is doing it silently, but forcefully and unambiguously.

This is a form of adequate, commonly understood and accepted communication. The child informs the adult of his feelings and intentions deliberately. The commanding adult can read these feelings and intentions in their finest nuances and gradations. He understands the message, and he will respond in kind, with a combination of words, expressive movements, and actions to which the child will respond in turn, and so on. An exchange of informative communications, with or without words, can thus take place.

When the mother asked the seven-year-old boy to accompany us upstairs, I expected him to react with such communication - not necessarily verbal. It could have been a gesture of anxiety and hesitation, or a smile of recognition and acceptance, or an expression of angry defiance, or any other emotional and therefore communicative reaction. The absence of such a reaction left me perplexed. Initially, I couldn't help but interpret this lack of response as if it were an intentional act, a message from him to his mother and me. During those few seconds, I hesitated between doubting that he expressed complete indifference to what was happening around him, or that he was merely feigning indifference, or that he might be telling us in his own way: "I'm not coming." The idea that he might be deaf also crossed my mind. However, as a psychiatrist and knowing his history, I also suspected that he might be autistic. This suspicion, "he might be autistic," was quickly confirmed. Johnny never communicated with us in any way, while his non-communicative action was comparatively adequate. We never exchanged a single word, never shared a smile. He would just turn away or withdraw with a blank and empty face whenever I tried to approach him. It was impossible to know what was going on inside him, and it was impossible to establish any form of relationship with him. The overall impression was: completely autistic.

Remember well: this impression of being "completely autistic" was not solely due to the fact that Johnny did not use words. There is a difference between the concept of "he doesn't speak" and the other "he doesn't communicate." This difference is important and needs to be examined more closely.

The behavior of Johnny and that of other children showing similar autistic behavior is usually described as "mutism." However, the difficulty of Johnny's "mutism," as observed during that hour, encompasses more than verbal language. This can be easily demonstrated by comparing Johnny's defect with that of a child suffering from cortical aphasia, or with that of a deaf child, or with the inability of a ten-month-old baby to express itself with words. All these children have in common that verbal language is not at their disposal. None of them can "speak." Yet, they communicate. They do so, often with great vigor, through another set of well-established and commonly understood symbolizations. These are the same as those used by the disobedient child in the example above. Here, we refer to the part of our language that includes all non-verbal, intentional, and communicative symbolizations: through expressive movements of the face and body, through expressive inarticulate sounds, and through the expressive modulation of spoken words in our language. These non-verbal symbolizations are available to any healthy person. They are an essential part of their language. They emit them - in a complex fusion with verbal language symbols - as long as they are in communication with people. These communicative symbolizations are not emitted by autistic individuals, nor by a healthy, solitary person, i.e., someone who is not in communicative contact with others.

The use of this set of symbolizations - facial expressions, bodily movements, and modulation of articulated and inarticulate sounds - is at least as characteristic of the state of non-autism as the use of spoken words. Indeed, the phenomenon of the absence of gestures and modulation of sounds, and especially the sight of a person's face remaining empty and expressionless in a situation where expressive movements are expected, essentially contributes to this overall impression of "he is autistic" that has been deemed so perplexing and inaccessible to psychopathological analysis.

This set of symbolizations - facial and bodily gestures, modulations of spoken language, and expressive inarticulate sounds - is older and more archaic in character than the language of words. It is governed by different brain centers. Therefore, it can continue to function in cases of typical aphasia when the cortical centers that control our verbal language are damaged or not yet developed. This set of non-verbal, communicative symbolizations - facial and bodily gestures, modulations of spoken language, and expressive inarticulate sounds - will be referred to as "affective language" from now on in this study. The total sum of all communicative verbal symbolizations will be subsumed under the term verbal language. Our everyday language is always a fusion and integration of verbal language and affective language.

We previously mentioned the social behavior of a ten-month-old baby who does not yet speak and of deaf or aphasic children as examples of the isolated existence of affective language. We want to briefly describe this phenomenon in a baby before it "learns to speak."

A healthy ten-month-old baby is certainly capable of telling its mother a lot about itself, even if it does not yet have articulated words at its disposal. It does so, if not with deliberate consciousness, then intentionally. Suppose it is now lying alone in its crib, awake, in peaceful contentment. Its mother comes to play with it. The moment it sees her and she addresses it, its previously expressionless face lights up. It smiles or laughs, coos, and its arms and legs move in an excited manner. All of this is not merely an autonomous motor release of its feelings of contentment and happy anticipation. It is also an intentionally directed message to its mother, conveying something like: "I'm so glad you've come to entertain me. Go ahead, move on!" The mother understands this well and responds to it in "baby language." It is true that she uses a few words. However, she doesn't really expect the baby to understand them. She primarily uses them as supports for something else, for the gestural movements and highly expressive sounds of this particular language.

The mother can now express with exaggerated gestures and exclamations her delight in seeing the baby in such good spirits. She may pick the baby up, kiss and caress it. To this, let's suppose, the baby responds with a defensive stiffening. Its face shows slight annoyance. The mother quickly reacts by putting it back in the crib and making soothing gestures and sounds. Peace is restored, the baby lies there, looking at its mother with an expression of searching and waiting. The mother teases and holds back for a moment, letting the baby wait. It understands and appreciates this playful extension of its pleasure. It responds by saying, "Come on, what are we waiting for!" It does so through gestures and sounds that are a delightful blend of seduction and joyful, eager impatience. The mother then performs an acrobatic move the baby hasn't seen before. The baby's face shows surprise, then intense concentration. It observes, then looks at its mother, emitting a well-modulated sound, almost as if asking, "So, what do we have here?" It watches her respond to that question, then replies with a little smile. Its gaze returns to the repetition of the small cascade. Suddenly, it bursts into hearty laughter, its face sparkling with joy, all its limbs in excited motion, kicking.

This is how it conveys to its mother, very adequately, its strong and relatively simple inner experiences. Each of them finds its correspondence in the non-verbal communicative symbols of movements and sounds. Words do not yet exist at this age, and they are not even necessary for what needs to be expressed.

These gestural expressions or inner experiences are genuine

symbols of communication. The same expression always represents the same inner experience. Moreover, these symbols have validity not only for this baby and its mother but also for the whole group to which these two individuals belong. They hold true within their family, within their country, and to some extent, worldwide, beyond the boundaries of the specific language of words that the baby will soon learn.

Each expressive movement and each expressive sound is a genuine symbol of communication. This also holds for them at a later stage in life when different patterns of non-verbal communication become more determined and even more specific than they are in baby language. A specific non-verbal expression is automatically used to express a specific inner experience. The same motor pattern observed in someone else is automatically understood as the expression of that inner experience.

Deaf children and young aphasic children are in a similar situation as babies before the development of speech. Being deprived of the language of words, they must depend compensatorily on the tool of their non-verbal language if they want to communicate with the people around them.

As inadequate as this substitute may be in many respects, especially when it comes to communicating factual, conceptual, and logical thoughts, it is certainly sufficient to maintain what we call "good contact with people." A rich and smooth flow of communication circulates between the healthy deaf child and the people they are in contact with. It is conveyed exclusively through the same means used in baby language: the non-verbal, expressive symbols of movements and sounds.

It seems appropriate at this point to give a first purely descriptive and very provisional definition of the term "autism" as it has emerged so far:

(1) a person who, at any given time, does not communicate their thoughts, feelings, and intentions to others is in a state of autism;

(2) if they persistently fail to communicate in situations where communication with others is expected and taken for granted, they must be considered pathologically autistic;

(3) the term "communicate," which, descriptively, is so closely linked to that of "autism," encompasses more than the mere ability to speak words and understand their symbolic meaning. It also requires, and particularly so, the use of this set of non-verbal, intentional, and communicative symbolizations, which can be collectively referred to as "affective language." It primarily serves to express affects, feelings, and emotions.

It is primarily this set of symbolizations - facial and bodily gestures, modulations of spoken language, and expressive inarticulate sounds - that conveys what we experience as "good contact with people." The "affective language," not verbal language, is the primary medium of this contact. In line with this, we can also expect a correlation between disturbances of affective language and disturbances of affective contact. In cases of extreme autism in early childhood, such as in the case described above of Johnny, we find that affective language has been practically extinguished along with verbal language. When approaching these children, we experience: no relationship can be established with them. Affective contact with them is completely interrupted.

Here we have - in purely descriptive terms - a basic symptomatology: extreme autism is equivalent to a profound interruption of any communicative relationship with people, resulting in a total extinction of all communicative and symbolic activities. Both verbal language and affective language have disappeared. Instead of being informed by the child about what is happening inside them, we have to rely on non-communicating signs and actions.

PART II: VERBAL LANGUAGE IN THE

AUTISTIC CONDITIONS OF CHILDHOOD

In Parts 2 and 3 of this chapter, we want to describe the different means of communication still available to autistic children or that they develop as substitutes. The fate of verbal language will be described in Part 2, and that of affective language in Part 3.

If we assume, and I believe it to be the case, that autism is characterized, among its many other qualities, by its degree, Case 1 certainly lies at one end of the scale. The interruption of communicative relationships is almost total. However, absolute autism, i.e., the complete rupture of all interpersonal relationships, is never found. Autistic children always show some signs of awareness of the people around them. In particular, the people on whom they depend for their daily needs and care are significant to them. They recognize the regular satisfactions and pleasures they offer. They expect their services to arrive at the right time and, in their own way, demand these services. They even cooperate in many of these activities, provided they are familiar to them and meet their regular needs. They react with violent affective outbursts when adults do not function as expected, causing painful disruptions to their daily routine and their hypersensitive perceptual system. One may wonder how sufficient understanding and cooperation for these purposes can be established when normal channels of communication are inaccessible or destroyed.

(1) Some understanding of spoken language

always preserved

We must immediately correct what we said in the last sentence of the previous paragraph. Some meager bridges or genuine communications are always preserved. In particular, spoken language is never completely annihilated. Children always have some understanding of spoken language - unless there is some other generally organic pathology in addition to autism - and their ability to speak is more or less intact, if only as a potentiality.

Let us examine once again the term "mutism." As it is usually used in psychiatric language, it seems to imply that a person does not speak, although hidden somewhere, in one way or another, their ability to speak exists. This phrase "he is mute," as it is used to describe completely autistic children, even carries a slight accusatory flavor of "he could if he wanted to" and "he refuses to speak." After all, parents as well as the psychiatrist know from immediate experience (as described in Case I) that the child understands at least part of what is said within their reach. Sometimes, through their non-communicative actions, one can see that they have taken note of what has been said to them. In other frequent cases, one can see from their reaction that they have understood but are compelled to reject the intrusion as something painful or unpleasant. This is done either through an absolute lack of reaction, at which many of these children excel, or through an active and negative counter-impulse. Of course, very often, the autistic child perceives nothing at all in their autistic seclusion. It should be emphasized that these three mechanisms - not perceiving, perceiving but not reacting, and reacting with a negative counter-impulse - are customary, automatic, and compelling. These three mechanisms are closely interconnected, and they cannot even be clearly separated from one another, as there exist fluid forms of transition between them. Certainly, it is not necessary to point out here that the autistic child cannot help but react as they do, so the term "compulsive" is defensible here, provided it is taken in its literal sense, and not in the usual sense of the psychiatric diagnosis "compulsive-neurotic."

(2)   Occasionally,   genuine   verbal communications emanate from the autistic child

These are cases where even extremely autistic children actually speak. It was mentioned that Johnny (Case I) could say a few words occasionally, always under the pressure of a strong need or desire that forced him to break out of his isolation and compelled him to overcome the barrier of his negativism. He could then make a visibly significant effort and formulate requests in one or two words such as "Coca!", "Ice cream!", "Open door!", "No!" and several others. These were the rare occasions in his life when he was truly communicative, meaning that he addressed words to other people with the intention of conveying meaning and being understood. During these moments, he could not be described as "autistic." Similar momentary interruptions of autism are reported in many extremely autistic children.

(3) Verbal productions by heart

The well-known rote verbal productions of chronic autistic children, resembling parrots, belong to a different category. They should not be mistaken for genuine communication, whether the child knows what they are saying or not (in some cases, they do know, in others, they don't, and in some cases, it is unclear whether they know or not). These productions, of which we intend to provide several examples, serve to demonstrate once again that the ability to speak, to utter words, is preserved in autistic conditions of childhood or - to be more cautious - it is only damaged to an uncertain degree. Parents may insist with some justification: "He can talk. Yes, he can, as long as it is nothing more than the rote recitation of words and word combinations, more or less organized, and to some extent, understanding their symbolic meaning. However, the mere utterance of words and phrases does not equate to communication. Addressing a person is an important aspect of communicative language. A healthy child reciting a poem monotonously at school is not communicating, no more than an autistic child who, under appropriate stimulation, automatically sings or recites an entire song or story exactly as they have heard it.

Without considering these facts, one cannot grasp the meaning of the various vocalizations and verbalizations of children who suffer from autism less extreme than Johnny's. These children use words, as well as gestures and modulated sounds in a manner that resembles human language but appears peculiar. Indeed, language, when used for purposes other than communication, seems strange. Here are some examples, still within the realm of extreme pathology, even if one cannot speak of complete autistic mutism anymore.

<u>Case II</u>

A ten-year-old boy, whom we'll call Dick, has been deeply autistic for many years and is engrossed in the playroom with a game consisting of monotonously moving toy furniture from the dollhouse to a nearby table. He takes one toy after another, touches it, gazes at it for a few seconds, brings it close to his nose, and smells it. Then he adds it to the other pieces already piled up on the table. This repetitive procedure continues for about twenty minutes. Dick remains in deep silence, and his face shows no expression throughout this time. Attempts to speak to him or engage in communication with him are futile. He seems to pay no attention to the observer or his mother, who sits in a corner of the room. However, the observer soon learns that this impression is not entirely accurate. After some time, it becomes apparent that Dick sometimes makes efforts to approach the observer, who is sitting away from the table. On two occasions, he even brushes against the observer's knees with his body. The observer is still unsure whether this behavior is accidental or intentional because Dick's expression remains blank and indifferent on each occasion.

Suddenly, Dick interrupts his game, comes very close to the observer, and scrutinizes the various parts of the observer's face. The two faces almost touch. Dick does this with an entirely detached expression, as if the observer's face were an interesting but inanimate object that he gazes at casually. However, his eyes suddenly widen, and his movements become more tense, indicating that "he might be excited or anxious." The observer had undergone this same strange examination in the previous hours. The first time, he had smiled awkwardly when Dick's eyes fixated on him so closely. The negativistic mechanism had immediately triggered. Dick withdrew and turned away hurriedly. In subsequent instances, the observer managed to keep his face calmly friendly and non-aggressive. This allowed Dick to satisfy his curiosity and then return to stacking the doll furniture at his own pace. Finally, the last piece of furniture was taken out of the dollhouse. A brief period of indecision followed. Dick's hands explored the interior of the dollhouse for a moment. Then he turned back to the doll furniture on the table. For a while, he resumed picking up the furniture, looking at it, touching it, smelling it, and then placing it back.

Something new eventually happened. With a quick arm movement, he knocked a few toys from the table to the floor. Dick might have done it intentionally or accidentally; his face remained blank while doing so. It was only when the same action was repeated a second and third time that it became evident he had done it deliberately. The action was followed each time by a few spastic motor discharges, which are frequently observed in autistic children in response to pleasurable and exciting experiences. When the pieces fell to the floor with some noise, he jumped in place for a few moments, vigorously shaking his arms and hands.

At this point, Dick's mother intervened. She ordered from her chair, "Pick it up, Dickie!" Dick reacted with a quick movement, as if he intended to comply. However, the intention was immediately halted by a negativistic counter-impulse. Dick turned away abruptly and resumed sweeping the toys from the table to the floor. He might have done it now with a mischievous intent. His expressionless face persisted.

Nevertheless, the strongly modulated sound sequence, "Pick it up, Dickie!" had an effect on Dick. After a while, he started to repeat the words with the same melody and pronunciation as his mother. From now on, he accompanied the toy handling with a repetitive chant of the two words: "Pick it up, pick it up, pick it up - - -." It did not sound mocking but rather like he was adding a pleasant little song to his work.

This last described event may be considered the prototype of many other cases where autistic children endlessly repeat words or word sequences simply because they perceive them as stimulating and enjoyable sound effects. Anyone who has worked with autistic children has experienced this many times. Here is another example.

Case III

A seven-year-old boy, extremely autistic, quite similar to the two children described above, except that he vocalizes more freely, enjoys listening to the radio at a certain time. Music has a stimulating and calming effect on him (as it does on the overwhelming majority of very young autistic children). This boy is particularly fascinated by the jingles and tunes from commercial radio. Their repetitiveness and strong modulation of words and melodies have an impact on him. In a way, he knows when his favorites will come on. He eagerly anticipates them with visible motor excitement and responds to their appearance with ecstatic motor discharges, jumping and shaking his hands and arms, as described earlier. Himself, when in a good mood, he reproduces these commercials by endlessly repeating them: "Buy Eversharp, buy Eversharp, - - -," and many others. He does it very well. The melody and accentuation of the little phrases or rhymes are perfectly imitated. The words are mutilated in a way that they can only be understood if one knows the corresponding advertisement. To him, they are just sounds that tickle him. He enjoys reproducing them without intending to convey meaning to others. The parents are proud of this accomplishment. They hope it's a first step toward relearning speech.

The emergence of such melodic and rhythmic vocalizations, often very precise and well-articulated, after months or years of complete mutism, gives rise to great hopes among parents. Finally, the child has started to talk. During their first meeting with the psychiatrist, they often make painful efforts to have the child perform these feats to convince the psychiatrist of their child's good memory and high intellectual potential. Some of these performances are truly remarkable. Difficult words, complex sentence structures, entire poems, and songs are recited with the most exact reproduction of insignificant details, especially regarding tone and accentuation. It's always the exact emphasis and modulation that the child originally heard. He cannot transform them into his own emotional language because he doesn't have one. The symbolic meaning not only of words but also of emotional language does not exist for him.

Only the pleasure of rhythm and melody remains.

(4) Verbal productions by heart are used as conditioned stimuli

However, these melodic and rhythmic vocalizations can have meaning in their own way. Let's consider the following example of the same boy (Case III). His father is accustomed to greeting him with an affectionate "Hi Baby" every evening when he returns home. Instead of responding to the meaningful content of this tender message with an equally affectionate reply (in his autistic way, he is very attached to his father), the boy repeats "Hi, Baby" several times, exactly reproducing the intonation of the exclamation. The casually affectionate tone of his father, when echoed by the son, seems truly bizarre. Billy's spasmodic jumps and the shaking of his arms and hands show that he enjoys it and also appreciates his father's response.

But there's more. After returning home in the evening, the father usually spends some time playing with Billy. These games are always physical and rough in nature. Billy is swung, tossed in the air, playfully boxed, tickled, etc. He loves it and has learned to demand it. He jumps in front of his father in wild anticipation and chants "Hi, Baby" when he wants to engage in rough play. He uses these two words for this purpose not only after the father's return home but also on other occasions when he wants to play with him. The father has learned to understand the meaning of these two words along with the jumping movements. In this situation, it means "Let's play!" The same two words take on a different meaning on another occasion, also related to the father's return home.

Billy often starts singing "Hi, baby" when he is waiting for and desiring his father's arrival, but the father is not coming. This is something new. It is no longer mere empty repetitions of sensually pleasing sound formations. Therefore, "Hi, Baby" has become a sign intentionally used to produce a specific effect. His parents, too, have learned to understand it in this way. They know the specific meanings of these two words in these two situations. For them, they have become genuine symbols.

Are they also symbols for Billy? Are we witnessing the emergence of a new language? And if we decide to call it language, what kind of language is it? We quickly realize significant differences between this use of the expression "Hi, baby" and the normal use of symbolic words. The two words mean something different for Billy and his parents than their usual meaning. In fact, the two words have taken on two different meanings in two different situations, both neologically different from the typical content of the two words "Hi, baby." These new meanings are extremely inflexible in specificity. There is not the slightest trace of generalization or categorization in them. The expression is used exclusively in these two precisely defined life situations, occurring regularly, and solely to provoke specific events - always exactly the same.

(5) Reflexive, Automatic Interaction, Stimulus-

<u>Response, without Language</u>

Before continuing our discussion on the use of the word "language" in childhood autism, we wish to describe another form of abnormal interaction regularly encountered between extremely autistic children and the people who care for them. The mechanism at work here also plays an important role in any normal interpersonal relationship. However, it often goes unnoticed because it is overshadowed and controlled by higher forms of communication and communicative action. It gains importance when these higher forms do not work, as is the case in childhood autism. In such cases, it becomes an important and sometimes very concerning symptom due to its compensatory overgrowth and because it appears in total isolation. The following case is an example of what we mean here.

<u>Case IV</u>

An eleven-year-old boy, profoundly autistic and, for all practical purposes, mentally disabled, moves around his room with his usual idle restlessness. His father, returning in the evening, appears at the door. The boy doesn't seem to pay attention to him. The father, too, stands there and waits with a calm and friendly expression. He has probably learned not to be aggressive with this child. Suddenly, without any other visible exchange, the boy stops in front of his father, slips his hand into one of the pockets of the father's coat, and takes the small gift that the father brings home every evening. He runs away with it. No notable communication takes place during this interlude. No smile, no expression of gratitude or pleasure is visible on the boy's face. Only an increase in his movements and some spasmodic motor discharges indicate to the observer that the boy experienced some pleasure. The father, too, remains there without saying anything. Yet, it can be seen that both understand each other in a certain way. This is regularly observed when deeply autistic children are observed in their daily lives: some form of substitute communication system exists between them and the people who regularly care for them. A primitive form of interaction is thus made possible despite the absence of words and gestures. The regularly repeated interactions become a private communication system themselves. This statement requires further explanation. Here is an example.

Case V

An autistic child is doing something in the psychiatric playroom for five minutes. His mother and the observer are watching him. Suddenly, the mother gets up, declares, "He needs to go to the bathroom," and urgently takes him there. The boy seems to expect it and even demand it. He willingly takes his mother's hand and runs with her. The observer had not noticed any signs indicating that the boy wanted to be taken to the bathroom. When asked about it later, the mother told the observer that she recognized certain agitated movements that indicated this particular need. The same boy was seen a few days later, this time without his mother. Suddenly, seemingly without reason, he burst into a violent affective crisis. He became restless, red, and sweaty, started whimpering, waving his arms in all directions, and finally hit his head as if in despair. Then he wet his pants. Undoubtedly, he had given the appropriate signals, well-known to his mother, and he expected the observer to have the appropriate and helpful reaction. It did not come because the observer was unable to understand. He later recalled that the affective outburst had been preceded by a certain change in motor behavior.

Case VI

A mother gets up from her chair (this was observed in the evening after dinner at the child's home) and walks across the room towards a closet. The child abruptly stops what he was doing. He rushes out of the room, ostentatiously putting himself out of her reach as quickly as possible. The mother is not disturbed. She seems to have anticipated it. She completes her course, which involves getting the child's pajamas from the closet. Then she proceeds with her other usual task of playfully and seriously chasing the boy. He waits for her in a distant corner of the house (it's always the same), jumping and dancing in excited anticipation of his mother's appearance. He starts running when she arrives. She chases him. Both seem to be having fun. He is quickly caught and taken to the bathroom for his usual bedtime ritual, after a somewhat superficial but vigorous struggle. The mother reports that this same interlude is an integral part of the bedtime routine.

Only a small part of the daily repeated activities between this autistic child and his mother has been described here. Both understood each other well. However, their method of conveying information to each other was fundamentally different from the usual method. It was not the generally accepted symbols of our language but individual stimuli, valid only in this particular context, that were used as cues for appropriate action. The mother's characteristic way of resolutely heading to the closet at that time of day was, for this boy, and for no one else, the signal that it was time for him to go to bed. The fact that the boy ran out of the room had become the signal for the mother to now chase and catch him before proceeding with the bedtime routine. Nothing other than these individually developed cues, and certainly not words or gestures, could do the job, as he was not receptive to them.

This is also true for the rest of the bedtime routine. It unfolded every day exactly the same way, with the mother and son performing the same rituals each time, thus giving each other the same signals in the correct sequence. This was the only way to allow this autistic child to orient himself and experience the security he was unable to derive from a living and overall understanding of the intentions of the people around him, as expressed by the symbols of our usual communication systems.

This explains the extreme rigidity and repetitiveness of many of these children's activities. The resemblance to compulsive-neurotic behavior is striking. Non-essential, external details of insignificant actions, petrified vestiges of once-meaningful partial actions, must be reproduced with photographic similarity each time at the same point, so that the respective activity can continue to progress correctly. The system is at risk of collapsing whenever one of these partial actions, or an appropriate response to one of them, does not occur. The child is suddenly disoriented. He no longer knows what to do and what will happen. He feels lost. A catastrophic reaction in the form of an outburst of autistic affect can quickly follow.

Now, let's return once again to the case of Billy (Case III) and the question of whether his particular use of the expression "Hi, baby" was genuine communication or not. We are now better able to understand the mechanisms behind it:

(1) Billy initially repeated those words for the simple sensual pleasure of their sound and rhythm;

(2) then, they became part of his daily routine, a part of the rigidly regulated and automated course of interaction between him and his father at night;

(3) from there, it was only a small but significant step for this partial action to become a specific and independent sign, used more or less deliberately to initiate a chain of actions, the play of the playhouse.

The "Hi, baby" used by Billy is no longer an automatic response to a rigidly prescribed stimulus. It has turned into a deliberate and intentional act.

It should not be surprising that Billy was able to take this step. After all, autistic children, even if intellectually impaired, are individuals and not mere brain preparations that function solely on an automatic stimulus-response basis. Besides their pronounced tendency to develop ritualized action patterns or conditioned reflexes, they are also capable of intentional acts of a voluntary nature. The "Hi, baby" used by Billy displayed the characteristics of such an intentional act. It appeared at moments chosen by Billy himself. He repeated it with growing urgency and with motor excitement that increased rapidly if his father did not respond promptly. He erupted into an outburst of affect if his efforts proved ineffective.

It is worth noting that the "Hi, baby" used by Billy was also a deliberate attempt to communicate his wish to another person. In a way, it was a genuine act of communication, even though language was used here in a very different way than the usual use of words.

Case VII

Here is another example, in many respects similar to the previous one.

A mother asks her autistic child at a certain time each day, "Do you want your orange juice now?" In doing so, she announces her intention to go to the kitchen and prepare this beverage for him. He has learned to understand it. He has also started using the same signal when he wants orange juice. He says with the same modulation and inflection of voice as his mother, "Do you want your orange juice now?" He expects this to result in the drink being made for him. His mother obliges. The same half-interrogative, half-suggestive phrase, when it comes from him, signifies a request and not a question or an offer.

The same mechanism as in "Hi, Baby" is operational here, except that a much more involved sentence structure has become a rigid sign in this case. The syntactic and grammatical inflexibility in using a whole sentence is surprising and remarkable. Many examples of this type can be found in young autistic children.

It seems that severe autistic children begin to learn or relearn to speak in this manner, with an initial period during which an inflexible, automated, stimulus-response language is developed, in conjunction with their other ritual behaviors. Everyday language, grammatically and syntactically flexible, which we consider natural, seems to develop only later. If it appears, it is probably at the same time as the development of conscious functions of conceptualization and categorization, recognition of causality and temporal and spatial relationships, and the development of logical thinking.

No healthy baby learns to speak in this way, rigidly echoing and repeating what they hear, with absolutely unchanged phrasing and syntax, and exactly imitating the expressive modulation of words and phrases heard. Babies inject something of their own into communication from the very beginning. They express themselves. They do so first with highly expressive gestures and sounds, then with isolated words, and finally with increasingly longer sentences. All these symbolizations, although initially heard and learned by watching and listening, are immediately incorporated and recreated as their own tools. This happens during the learning process itself, so newly acquired symbols are immediately used in a highly individualized form to express their feelings, desires, and later, thoughts about the person, object, or event in question. The gestures, sounds, words, etc. nevertheless remain the same linguistically understood and accepted symbols. Thus, everyone can understand what is expressed in a unique and highly individualized form. An admirable achievement, almost incomprehensible! We have all experienced it.

I don't think we have yet given enough thought, in psychopathology, to this difference we have just highlighted between a living response and a more or less thoughtful - automatic response. The former, the living response, has a unique form, never used before and never to be repeated, expressing what this person feels, thinks, wants, and intends to do in this new and never-to-be-repeated situation. The latter, the automatic response, is preformed. It is identical to its predecessors and successors in all its details and is triggered by a preformed stimulus that is always the same. The whole is a rigid and prefabricated reflex system that requires faithful repetition - the term "compulsive" would not be entirely correct here - of always the same situation.

It seems safe to conclude that the autistic child learns or relearns to speak in a fundamentally different way from that of a healthy baby, even though both methods converge towards the same ultimate goal, and even though we see intelligent autistic children achieve this goal. The most advanced among them learn to speak a conceptually and grammatically correct language, provided their autism does not completely cut them off from the people around them. The author of this article is not able to follow the development of autistic language through all its stages to its highest achievements, the excessively precise, overly logical, and overly objective language, grammatically and conceptually immaculate, as written and spoken by the occasional autistic child prodigy and schizoid adult genius. A continuum seems to extend between the two extremes, with Johnny from Case 1 representing one extreme, and the intellectually superior schizoid child representing the other.

We are familiar with this continuum, and we can indicate some of its common characteristics and some characteristic symptoms of certain phases of this continuum. However, most of the research in this area remains to be done. Such research should be profitable not only in providing new insights into the dynamics of schizophrenic development but also in giving us, by contrast, some indications of the development of our normal and everyday systems of communication and communicative symbolization.

PART III: THE AFFECTIVE LANGUAGE IN

AUTISTIC CONDITIONS OF CHILDHOOD

So far, in this chapter, we have described some of the stages through which a renaissance and a redevelopment of verbal language can take place after an autistic disruption of contact with people. We have limited ourselves to the broad outlines of this description. We have not done so merely by choice. Our knowledge and understanding of these restorative processes are still fragmentary and require further observations and clinical research.

In the third part of the following chapter, we will try to give a description - equally incomplete - of what happens to affective language in the different phases following an autistic breakdown of contact in childhood. It was shown in Case I that autistic mutism, unlike most other forms of language disorders, is characterized by the disappearance of verbal language along with affective language. Not only do the children not speak, but their faces also remain expressionless, and they fail to use expressive facial and bodily gestures, expressive sounds, and vocal modulations. They, therefore, do not communicate at all. The absence of any communicative symbolization gives them the impression of being alone and unaware of the people around them, even when they are among people and even when they are somehow acting in communion with them. It also makes them appear devoid of emotions and feelings.

The impairment of affective language is a more fundamental and significant symptom of autistic conditions in childhood than the impairment of verbal language. This statement, of course, goes hand in hand with the generally accepted hypothesis that - to express it in deliberately vague terms - the emotional sphere is more affected in autistic conditions than the intellectual sphere. However, this assertion has not been made solely based on theoretical considerations. It is the result of real observations of less damaged autistic children, those less completely cut off from the world. It has already been mentioned that these children can develop good verbal language. The most intelligent among them sometimes speak a particularly clear language, grammatically and otherwise immaculate. However, the deficit in affective language, or a certain deviation from it, persists even at the highest levels of intellectual performance. It is easy to recognize once one has learned to pay attention to it. Its symptoms are characteristic and well described.

So, here is an enumeration and an approximate and certainly incomplete description of some of these symptoms. We will attempt to show that affects and emotions manifest themselves in autistic conditions of childhood, even if they do not find expression in communicative symbolizations, and to show what efforts the child and the organism can make to reconstruct a new affective language.

(1) Affects and emotions can manifest through non-symbolic, non-communicative, motor, and neuro-hormonal expressions

The desperate affect explosions of extremely autistic children when their ritual activities are interrupted have been mentioned several times in this article. They can serve as a paradigm for what we have in mind when we say that autistic affects can make themselves known through their non-symbolic, non-communicative manifestations, even if the usual symbolic expression of the specific content and quality of the affect is lacking. You need to have seen these explosions to appreciate the unusual and bizarre aspect of such a violent motor, vasomotor and vegetative eruption, which is directed neither towards, nor against, nor away from anyone, and which gives no intentional information about the meaning and content of the affect. We are confronted with something that resembles an exceptionally strong explosion of affect, but whose symbolic and communicative parts have been strangely suppressed. Observing such an explosion, we realize that an affect is made up of two distinct but normally well-integrated parts, as far as its phenological manifestations are concerned: (1) the affect has its physical, reflective, neuro-hormonal components, and (2) it has its intentionally communicative and symbolic representation. The latter consists in giving information to another person (for whom the affect is intended) about its content: what provoked it, what is experienced and what is intended. Anger, for example, certainly has its neuro-hormonal manifestations. But we take it for granted that it's also about aggression against someone, firstly aggression through gestures, then less regularly aggression through words and physical attack, all expressed with the intention of letting the opponent know: I'm angry with you, I want revenge, I want to hurt you. In a fit of anger, you mock someone, show your fist, insult them, hit them, kick them or punch them. The opponent against whom the anger is directed is an essential part of it.

This intentional, expressive orientation towards another

person is absent from autistic affect. We see a child who, after a short period of non-specific motor agitation, suddenly finds himself in extreme motor and neuro-hormonal agitation. He screams or moans, emitting bizarre, monotonous sounds, but nothing is said or expressed; he shakes his limbs in violent motor discharges, but attacks no one; his face, bright red or livid, and covered in perspiration, is contorted, yet it's blank and stares at no one. The child frequently strikes his head with his fists or bangs it forcefully against the floor or wall. This has been interpreted, rightly or wrongly, as aggression turned against himself. Anyone who witnesses the event cannot doubt that the child is in desperate pain. We feel a strong sense of sympathy, all the more so because we don't know how to help him. Unless we know enough about his habits, we can't know what caused this unexpected outburst. We can't even know what kind of affect it is. The child may be in pain, he may have suddenly lost his orientation, he may be frightened or panicked, he may be angry. He may need specific help. He may want to eat or drink something, he may have wanted to be stroked or play one of his favorite games and not been satisfied, he may have had illusory or hallucinatory experiences. We can't know. He doesn't say so, and he doesn't express it any other way. This is a truly autistic outburst of affect.

Here's a description of another manifestation of autistic affect, this time in response to intense pain: a six-year-old girl, chronically autistic, was seen for the first time in the psychiatrist's office. This girl could speak, in a slow automaton-like language (her language will be described later). At one point during this interview, the psychiatrist spoke with her parents as she stood by the window, radiating a status-quo-like immobility. Suddenly, she began to moan, or rather, a long, monotonous moan escaped from her otherwise motionless and inexpressive body. A few seconds later (which is a long time on such an occasion!), she managed to take a small step away from the window and thus also from the hot radiator that had burned her leg. Finally, she was able to tell her mother what had happened. She had second-degree burns. The radiator was very hot, but certainly not enough to cause physical damage to a child with normal reflex defenses against pain. At first, none of us knew what had happened. Nothing was expressed in his affect.

Most manifestations of autistic affect are less violent and less spectacular than those just described. Since their symbolic and communicative component is absent, and reflective, motor and neuro-hormonal changes are often discreet, they easily go unnoticed unless we are familiar with the child's reactions in a familiar environment. This may be the child's home, an institutional setting or the psychiatric playroom where the child has been a regular visitor for some time. Slowly, we begin to notice the many small manifestations of affect that occur in the course of daily routine. You even learn to differentiate their significance. You learn to pay attention to small, sudden changes in his motor behavior, to a barely perceptible acceleration in the rhythm of his movements, to suddenly appearing movements of agitation, to a small blush on his face, to sudden changes in the posture and tone of his body, and in the autistic expression on his face. It's amazing how these little signs have their own specificity, so that it's possible to roughly predict what's coming next, once he dislikes something and gets angry, another time he gets impatient and is ready to destroy or take revenge, a third time he repeats himself for one of his light-hearted, mischievous acts. During all this time, no real communication takes place.

A very characteristic manifestation of affect is particularly frequent in childhood autistic states. This is a particular form of motor discharge in response to feelings of satisfaction, be it anticipated pleasure, or the actual experience of something pleasurable, or the satisfaction of an accomplishment, e.g. when the child has built something to his liking, or when he enjoys the effects of one of his little mischievous acts, and so on. This is a typical manifestation of autistic affect in that it is not directed at any person, and can be observed whether the child is in the presence of people or not. The child stands before the object of the scene or its satisfaction, body rigidly erect, head lowered to chest, arms and hands raised to the side of the body or in front of the shoulders, as very young children are often seen holding their arms while walking. In this very tense posture, he executes a series of staccato jumping movements ("pogo stick" movements) on the spot, while violently and spasmodically waving or shaking his hands. The face has a tense, orgasmic expression during this time. An example of such an event was given in Case II.

(2) Some feelings and emotions are implicitly expressed in the interaction between the child and the caregiver

It might suffice to give just one example of what is meant here. Many extremely autistic children enjoy intensive caresses, rough play, or any other playful and intense physical interaction. Of course, this must be done on their terms, at the moment they expect it, and it must be precisely that specific activity to which they are responsive. Furthermore, they usually can only receive attention and rarely give it. Their feelings are expressed implicitly through their actions. No overt communicative exchange takes place during the interaction.

The procedure may go as follows: a mother somehow realizes, based on her autistic child's behavior, that he would like to be taken on her lap and caressed. The child may express this simply by crawling towards her while she is sitting in front of him. She receives him kindly. He nestles against her body and within the safety of her arms, relaxes, and begins to suck his thumb happily. He appears to be in a state of profound peace, akin to nirvana. After a while, he has had enough. He then simply releases himself from her arms, gets off her lap, and leaves. His face remained expressionless and indifferent throughout this interlude.

Signs of impatience quickly appear if she attempts to keep him after he has had enough of the caresses. The affect is recognizable solely through his behavior and the accompanying neuro-hormonal reactions. He struggles to free himself from her embrace, his movements becoming more and more agitated. If she persists, he may quickly enter one of the violent affective outbursts described earlier.

Physical defense and struggle, flight, acts of destruction – all of these are generally the result of some affect (irritation, annoyance, fear, anger). Normally, one immediately witnesses the affect's development until it reaches its peak. The child expresses what is happening and communicates it to their partner or adversary. Hence, one is always warned in advance of what is about to happen. In the relationship with a severely autistic child, one is very often confronted with reactions such as sudden and violent struggle, unexpected retreat or flight, a destructive act that emerges suddenly from nowhere. Only through these actions can one deduce after the fact what the child might have felt. The respective feelings or emotions have not been expressed. I don't think it is necessary to emphasize this point further.

(3) A pseudo-affective language is developed

Here we directly refer to the "schizoid" child, meaning the child who can sufficiently use their intellectual powers and maintain a speech relationship with people, even though their contact with others has been interrupted or significantly weakened for a long period or perhaps throughout their life. They can verbally communicate with others, and they can even engage in conversations, as long as the subject aligns with their unilateral autistic interests.

As we have mentioned several times before: what they say can be very clear and well-articulated, formulated with excellent grammar (or they may exhibit symptoms of autistic language distortion). However, when listening and observing this "schizoid" language, one cannot help but notice that something is amiss (beyond the subtle or extensive pathology of its content). It becomes apparent that its second component remains defective or, more frequently, has developed insidiously.

Indeed, a semblance of affective language appears to develop in any chronic, prolonged, or permanent schizoid state as part of the organism's or individual's compensatory efforts. The very strange phenomenon of a complete disappearance of affective expression while the individual remains capable of conveying the content of their thoughts through verbal symbols is only observed in occasional acute catatonic states and (for different pathological reasons) in the Parkinsonian syndrome. In those instances, one can truly witness people speaking from a rigidly immobile face resembling a mask rather than a living countenance, from a rigidly immobile body resembling a statue rather than a living body, and they may speak in that soft, completely unmodulated, and monotonous language that we postulate as a complete and isolated detection of affective language.

Most schizoid children are aware or feel that something is wrong with them. Some of them are acutely aware that their experiences are incomplete or different from those of other people. Others deduce from the attitudes of the people around them that something is missing in their behavior and actions. They then make more or less conscious efforts to recover and redevelop what they believe they lack, trying to provide what they think is expected of them. Quite regularly, they attempt to retrieve their affective language as they see and notice it in others. This effort is doomed to failure because genuine affective language can only exist if it genuinely represents authentic feelings and emotions. The two main symptoms of chronic disorders of contact in childhood, regarding affective language, are therefore the following: (1) deficiency and (2) artificiality. The well-known empty, expressionless, and closed face and gaze of the schizoid child while speaking with someone can serve as a central example of the first quality of affective language mentioned: deficiency. The well-known schizoid and schizophrenic mannerisms are prototypes of its second quality: artificiality.

Signs of defective or artificial sound modulation are particularly common in children with chronic contact disorders. Typical language patterns emerge, which are sufficiently typical to serve as diagnostic signals. If one hears a child speak according to the described pattern, it appears familiar in relation to previous cases, and one thinks: an autistic child.

In the following, we will try to name and describe some of these patterns. However, it is essential to understand that the terms used here aim to describe rather than exhaustively classify. Moreover, mixtures between different types are the rule rather than the exception. That is the fate of any typological characterization, after all.

Besides (a) completely unmodulated, completely monotonous language, which no longer needs description, we want to mention here (b) "automaton language," (c) "scanning language," and (d) "declamatory language."

(b) Automaton language

This type of autistic language always appears to be a hallmark of a very severe pathology in the domain of affective contact, even if verbal and action-based contact can be maintained. Rather than describing this language abstractly, we want to illustrate it by describing the way a six-year-old girl with a schizophrenic condition (Case VIII) spoke and behaved. Trying to analyze my impression of her speaking, "She talks as one would expect an automaton to speak," I realize that this impression is very complex, encompassing not only her language but also her entire motor behavior and way of acting. Most of the time, she was stiff and immobile like a wax figure, and her rare actions were merely temporary and conspicuous interruptions of this state of immobility. These actions were also limited to the parts of her body immediately involved – her legs when walking, her hands and arms when writing or drawing. The rest of her body remained in its catatonic rigidity.

Occasionally, a speaking voice emerged from this immobile body. "Docteur Frankl, je veux dessiner." (Doctor Frankl, I want to draw.) This was her habitual response when the psychiatrist asked her at the beginning of the session what she wanted to do today. She responded only after the psychiatrist had conveyed to her several times and insistently that he genuinely wanted her to decide for herself what she wanted to do. Even then, it required significant effort on her part to overcome the powerful forces that hindered her intentionality. Sometimes, you could see from certain movements of her mouth that she intended to say something, but she had to repeat herself several times before successfully translating her intention into action.

The psychiatrist had become accustomed to waiting quietly after asking her such a question. A considerable time, sometimes certainly ten or fifteen seconds, would pass before an answer came. Nothing visible happened in the meantime. This made one feel like giving up on waiting for a response, either by repeating the question or, even worse, moving on to something else.

"Doc--tor--Frankl--I--want--to--draw". This phrase came out slowly, syllable by syllable, each one individually, clearly enunciated and strongly accented. Each syllable had exactly the same volume and pitch. The result was an especially inert impression, akin to that of a ghost. Occasionally, she could speak with a bit more spontaneity. The automaton-like character of the language persisted, but it was somewhat less laborious and a bit more fluid. For example, after finishing one of her drawings to her satisfaction, she would always draw the psychiatrist's attention to it: "Je veux que vous le voyiez." (I want you to see it.) The psychiatrist would then admire it and ask her about the meaning of the drawing. In response to that, she would provide the appropriate explanation, which always belonged to a story she had imagined about herself. On such occasions, she spoke more rapidly, reciting monotonous streams of words and syllables as if rehearsing a chain of thoughts she often ruminated on. She never managed to say more than two or three sentences in a row before interrupting herself and falling back into her catatonic immobility.

To avoid misunderstandings, it is essential to note that this same girl had a very proficient verbal language. She could express herself through writing and drawing with a great deal of artistic intuition. At one point, she wrote a long story illustrated with elaborate drawings, arranged in the form of a book. Its content, concerning a girl, her father, and her brother, was highly symbolic. Nevertheless, it strongly conveyed her own feelings, frustrations, and resentments within her family.

The reader may have noticed that we have described here a state and language that would be qualified as catatonic if it were an adult case. The combination of profound impairment in affective contact with people and equally profound impairment in intentional action characterizes the clinical picture. The author of this article knows only one other case of this kind in childhood, that of a preadolescent girl who combined the same automaton-like language with a rigidity of the body similar to that of catatonia. The first case has remained stationary for many years now, and the second had a progressive nature, with a slow but perceptible deepening of the schizophrenic state over the years.

(c) "Sweeping" language

This type of language is frequently heard in chronic childhood contact disorders, especially in slightly schizoid personality disorders during latency, preadolescence, and adolescence. Its particular rhythmic monotony is easily recognizable once one has learned to pay attention to it, making it serve as a diagnostic clue or marker when the child utters their first words or phrases in the presence of the psychiatrist.

This language is characterized by a monotonous rhythm instead of complete homogeneity of volume and pitch. "La racine carrée de seize est quatre." (The square root of sixteen is four.) The emphasized syllables are drawn out and heavily accented in a monotone chant, while the unaccented syllables are all short and soft. The most important word or syllable in the sentence generally receives a particularly heavy and long, drawn-out accent. The rhythmic changes in pitch and volume are monotonously the same from one phrase to another. The overall impression is that of a very rhythmic language, but devoid of life and emotion. There is a certain resemblance to the activity of scanning the lines of poetry without considering their content.

An effort to retrieve, if not an affective modulation of speech, at least a modulated structure of speech is made here. However, this structure highlights the grammatical, logical, and conceptual values of the discourse's content rather than conveying feelings and emotions. Consequently, this manner of speaking is often heard in over-intellectualizing schizoid children, especially when discussing those highly circumscribed, abstract, sometimes very original and valuable, and sometimes obscure and ritualistic domains of interest in which these children often specialize.

(d) "Declaiming" language

The author of this article vividly remembers a scene in which a ten-year-old boy, clearly schizoid (Case IX), described his experiences with measles. It was already a few weeks after he had

had the disease. He stood in front of the listener, his eyes fixed on the floor, his expressionless face reddening with excitement as he narrated, occasionally with a trace of autistic smile when relishing particularly sensational parts of his story.

It was a highly dramatic narrative of events that, from an objective point of view, were rather uneventful. "--- and you know what, Miss X? I woke up in the middle of the night, and my whole body was hot and itchy." He continued to describe in the same manner how his head hurt and how he felt nauseous. He imitated his mother's actions, and he vividly recalled how she exclaimed, "Oh my God, measles." She took his temperature, and he reproduced her horrified cry, "Oh my God, one hundred and six point ten."

Listening to this story, one is reminded of the way fairy tales, especially in their most important parts, are told to young children. The excessive dramatization was achieved through exaggerated inflections of the voice, enormous rises and falls in volume and pitch that, in their entirety, resembled an exaggerated theatrical performance rather than a genuine expression or reproduction of feelings and emotions. Characteristically, he reproduced his and his mother's experiences in this event without making any distinction between them.

In the case of well-developed declaiming language, the child usually speaks as if reciting a poem or story, with an overly sentimental or dramatic overexpression of emotions and feelings, and with excessive emphasis on what would be emphasized anyway. If all of this were genuine, it would reflect very strong emotions and feelings. However, the listener does not experience it as an authentic and immediate expression of affect. In some cases, it resembles a poor manneristic imitation of someone else's affect expression, in others, a good histrionic performance, and in others, the reproduction of emotional experiences that were once lived and are now reflected upon. Very often, one hears only an empty, habitual chant with overly strong but repetitive and meaningless affective inflections that only faintly resemble genuine affective language. They bear the poignant testimony of the child's more or less conscious efforts to reclaim the feelings of others, to speak and express themselves as they hear others do.

AFTERWORD

In order to explain and comment precisely on George Frankl's thoughts, I will organize this preface into three dates, although some of the ideas and reasoning are evolutionary and go beyond the initial dates.

1934:

"Normal" people communicate much more about the form (the way of saying) than the content (the meaning of words), and thus engage in subjective communication. They adapt the message and form based on the person receiving the communication, their personality, temperament, and emotional state (if the person is sad, fearful, etc.). Also, they modify the form of communication and the message based on their opinion and feelings about the person who will receive the message (if the person is angry or dislikes the person in front, for example). Since "normal" people focus their communication on the form, they are more sensitive to social elements such as social roles, titles, and hierarchies. Consequently, they expect specific responses and reactions based on these factors. They perceive, experience, and interpret any deviation from these expected responses and behavior as an affront, lack of respect, or consideration. Therefore, in such cases, they may alter their behavior and the form of communication in response, leading to communication problems and conflicts.

To communicate effectively and constructively with autistic

individuals, neurotypical individuals must communicate objectively and impersonally. Therefore, scolding, reprimanding, threatening, and ordering are futile as rules of order-obedience do not work and are counterproductive, often yielding opposite effects. It is also pointless to convey the message in form rather than content, as it is not understood. Conversely, neurotypicals do not comprehend how an autistic individual may focus on the message's content rather than the form, which leads to mutual misunderstandings.

These rules and observations are general and may seem "caricatured." It also means that some autistics can adapt to form-focused neurotypical language, and neurotypicals can use content-focused language. However, this explains the common reproaches directed at autistics for being "too cold" and at neurotypicals for "not saying what they really mean."

It is advised to use impersonal and concrete language and behavior (without abstraction or implications) with autistics. This way, the autistic individual will feel respected and appreciated appropriately. This implies that the person interacting with an autistic individual must be unconditional and consistently exhibit behaviors, attitudes, and dispositions (psychological, cognitive, and affective). Asperger wrote in 1944 that in an educational relationship with children, instructions should not be "announced as personal requests but as objective and impersonal laws." (Rebecchi, 2023a, p. 49). This can be explained by the fact that an impersonal and concrete instruction follows rules and laws rather than the arbitrariness or emotion of the person issuing it (e.g., "It's time to brush your teeth," implying it happens at the same time every day, versus "Go brush your teeth," implying an arbitrary decision). In the first case, the child will often comply without objection, whereas in the second case, they may "disobey" and display negativism. Thus, in the context of communication with an autistic child, everything hinges on the adult's communication, which can create either a serene or chaotic atmosphere. Moreover, being impersonal does not mean being cold and detached, but it does mean not offering or expecting signs of affection or friendship.

Therefore, the change in attitude and language will not "cure" the autistic individual, but it will allow them to adapt socially, through a marketing and communication principle that is highly valued by neurotypical humans: "communicating while adapting to the target." This may seem destabilizing to the majority of individuals, but it simply involves updating one's cognitive software to act and communicate differently, something that autistics naturally do from birth to death.

1943:

George Frankl states that human language is composed of verbal language and affective and emotional language. According to him, autistic individuals suffer from a "lack of contact with people," as, even though they have a human appearance and often behave like humans, they lack a singular human ability: the capacity to communicate and engage in social relationships with others.

According to him, the "disorder" lies in the view and sentiment of neurotypicals that the autistic individual does not react as they expect. He explains that in "healthy" individuals (including

149

the deaf-mute, aphasic, mentally challenged, Parkinson's patients, etc.), there is a communicative tendency and a desire to establish and maintain relations with people and communities. Furthermore, he notes that the autistic's impairment of affective contact is opposite to the impairment of verbal contact in deficient individuals, and thus, this lack of affective communication should never be interpreted as a lack of intelligence. Finally, he emphasizes that affective gestures and behaviors are not abandoned relics of prehistory but still play a crucial role in human communication today.

1957:

Thus, according to Frankl, autism can be seen as a specific mindset and not as something abnormal; in other words, it is a "condition." He raises the question of the emergence of a new language and its type, which does not necessarily rely on speech and allows the creation of intimate and private communication systems composed of elements applicable to specific contexts, enabling the exchange and provocation of specific actions and reactions. Ultimately, it would be a (very) different way of using language and words, but one that still allows communication. The form of this language sometimes appears invisible to an untrained and profane eye (isn't it the same in Star Trek and Lord of the Rings with telepathy?), and it is fundamentally different from the usual language. However, like the latter, it converges towards the same goal of communication and interaction. Thus, what is typically interpreted as a withdrawal from social contact or the sociocultural world should rather be understood as an absolute lack of pursuit of human contact and socialization as the main and essential activity of the individual. The autistic individual has their own environment and way of seeing, perceiving, and understanding people and things, and it is this difference in mindset, condition, and cognition (different from the usual mindset, which is all about social connection and conforming to norms at all costs to be integrated into a group) that causes this pathologization of the difference, which is, in reality, due to ignorance and misunderstanding.

Frankl also mentioned a continuum of autistic conditions, extending from Kanner's autism (Rebecchi, 2023b) to Asperger's autism (Rebecchi, 2023a), passing through Sukhareva's autism (Rebecchi, 2022). In all cases, the emotional and affective sphere would be much more "affected" than the cognitive and intellectual sphere.

Furthermore, autistic verbal language is often very profound at the semantic level, sometimes referred to as hyperpedantry of language (Beaud & De Guibert, 2011). Autistic emotional and affective explosions often lack communicative meaning in the usual sense. For example, a neurotypical person in anger might be aggressive in gestures, words, and even physically, seeking revenge, harm, ridicule, insults, or violence. In contrast, an autistic person in anger might simply say they are angry, direct their anger inward, or say nothing at all, not explicitly expressing their emotions. Hence, sometimes tools are introduced to help autistic individuals communicate their emotions in ways similar to neurotypicals, or social skills groups are designed to understand neurotypical social language. But shouldn't, for the sake of equity and social justice, tools be implemented to help neurotypicals (not just professionals) communicate their emotions in the way autistic individuals do and create social skills groups to understand autistic (social) language? Wouldn't that be the realization of a respectful society that takes into account the concept of neurodiversity?

In conclusion, Frankl perfectly described the problems of double empathy - reflecting the idea that neurotypicals and neuroatypicals struggle to understand each other in both directions (Milton, 2012; Crompton et al., 2021) - and the inefficiency of communication between neurotypicals and neuroatypicals, not because autistic individuals have deficits or disabilities, but because they naturally develop a different way of communicating based on content (meaning) rather than form, while neurotypicals develop a way of communicating based on form (affective) rather than content (meaning). This explains the hyperprecision in autistic individuals' vocabulary versus the emotional undertones in neurotypical language, which may sometimes appear as hypocrisy, manipulation, or lying to uninitiated autistic individuals.

Isn't it because neurotypicals master this type of language and create norms and rules that they pathologize anything exceptional? Isn't the language of autistic individuals rather rational and efficient in everyday life situations? Have we ever seen another animal species use a language wrapped in affect rather than focusing on meaning? Wouldn't that be dangerous in nature? This is also why communication among autistic individuals is so effective (Crompton et al., 2020) as it is informative and explicit primarily. Is this ultimately the real purpose of communication?

The most surprising aspect of this situation is the conditioning of autistic individuals, leading them to analyze their own way of communicating in a pathological manner. However, the strategy of pathologizing a language difference could easily be reproduced in the opposite direction. Are there really no communication problems among neurotypicals? Then, what explains the wars and diplomatic incidents that have lasted for millennia? Isn't the neurotypical "Instagram" language a symptom, the visible part of a society based on appearance and form, where depth, precision, and substance are only marginally valued, and any deviation from these rules is punished?

References

Beaud, L., & De Guibert, C. (2011). Identité et spécificité du « pédantisme » dans le syndrome d'Asperger. Neuropsychiatrie de l'enfance et de l'adolescence, 59, 469–477. https://doi.org/10.1016/j.neurenf.2011.09.004

Crompton, C. J., DeBrabander, K., Heasman, B., Milton, D., Sasson, N. J. (2021) Double Empathy: Why Autistic People Are Often Misunderstood. Frontiers for Young Minds, 9. https://doi.org/10.3389/frym.2021.554875

Crompton, C. J., Ropar, D., Evans-Williams, C. V., Flynn, E. G., & Fletcher-Watson, S. (2020). Autistic peer-to-peer information transfer is highly effective. Autism, 136236132091928. https://doi.org/10.1177/1362361320919286

Milton, D. (2012) On the ontological status of autism: the 'double empathy problem', Disability & Society, 27:6, 883-887. http://doi.org/10.1080/09687599.2012.710008

Rebecchi, K. (2022). Autistic children: Grunya Sukhareva. Kindle Direct Publishing.

Rebecchi, K. (2023a). Autistic children: Hans Asperger. Kindle Direct Publishing.

Rebecchi, K. (2023b). Autistic children: Leo Kanner. Kindle Direct Publishing.